THIS BOOK BELONGS TO:

....

Let's Be Friends

Calyn Daniel
Blythe Daniel

HARVEST HOUSE PUBLISHERS
EUGENE, OREGON

Published in association with The Blythe Daniel Agency, Inc., www.theblythedanielagency.com.

Cover design by Emily Weigel Design
Cover photo © Akbaly (border); 2d collection (BFF bracelet) / Shutterstock
Interior design by Janelle Coury

For bulk, special sales, or ministry purchases, please call 1-800-547-8979.
Email: Customerservice@hhpbooks.com

Let's Be Friends

Copyright © 2023 by Calyn Daniel and Blythe Daniel
Published by Harvest House Publishers
Eugene, Oregon 97408
www.harvesthousepublishers.com

ISBN 978-0-7369-8810-0 (pbk.)
ISBN 978-0-7369-8811-7 (eBook)

Library of Congress Control Number: 2023934553

Printed in the United States of America

23 24 25 26 27 28 29 30 31 / BP / 10 9 8 7 6 5 4 3 2 1

This book is dedicated to moms who want their daughters to have best friends, including our mom and Nannie—Helen McIntosh—who has shown us what it looks like to speak affirming words and grow in your friendships as you honor and respect others.

To all the girls who are looking to find friends who will remain true, this book is for you as you seek and become a best friend! May you know your full worth and value and remember that you deserve friends who love and embrace you as you travel this season of life together.

CONTENTS

BONUS FEATURES

Welcome

Hello there! We're so glad that you are seeking to make friends. Do you wish for that one special, best friend? Even a circle of friends who you can share fun moments and memories with? This book is just for you! You are special to God, and He is the best friend you could ever have. He will never disappoint you even when others do.

He wants to use YOU in your friendships to be a positive influence on others. And we want to cheer you on and celebrate what a good friend you are and encourage you as you make new friends.

So hey! You are in the exact place that God wants you to be. He has called you to be a friend who loves others even with their flaws and to know that you are loved just as you are. Even if right now you don't have the best friend you hope to have, we want to share some ways you can seek good friends in your life.

We are a mom, Blythe (who remembers being your age!), and a daughter, Calyn (who gets you!), sharing our hearts with you. We know that it's important for girls to believe that God is our number one go-to when it comes to friendships.

He never changes, even when friends do. God wants you to remember that you carry gifts in your heart to share with others. He gave you those gifts, and he can bring great friends into your life to share your heart, gifts, and time with. You are worth the investment of time a friend spends with you and you with them.

In this book we want you to think about making and keeping strong friendships. We hope you see yourself as someone who is making good choices and great friends. We have provided places throughout this book for you to write your thoughts and prayers for your friends, as well as a space at the end for you to remember what your friends have said about you and find some ways you can create memories together.

You've got so much to give to others! God looks at you with deep joy for his good creation of you. And he wants you to share the hope you have in him with your friends. We invite you to see what God can do in your life through the friends you choose. Friends who inspire and love you rather than bring you down.

The gift of who you are and the gift of friends make life sweeter. And God has made you to share your life with others. So as you turn the pages, we want to say, "Let's be friends!" and encourage you to pass on these thoughts to friends you have now and friends you will have in the future.

Calyn and Blythe

Fitting In

Have you ever tried on a pair of jeans and said to yourself, "These don't fit"? Sometimes friendships can feel like this. You want to know that you fit with others. You want to find your place with a friend or group of friends you can grow close with. You want to know that you can have a strong friendship together and that you have common interests. Do you know there is no one who can take your place? You fill a space no one else can!

We go through times when we don't feel like we fit in. You may feel that your friends are going in a certain direction and you're stuck not knowing whether to follow them or go your own way. You wish someone would just tell you what they like about you. You wonder if you have standout qualities.

Do you know how God sees you? He believes you are so special, and he made a really big effort to show you. He looks at you with a Father's love as if to say, "That's my girl. She is my creation, and I've done everything to make sure she knows how loved she is."

Have you thought about how Eve, the first woman God created, had to first learn how much God really loved her? She didn't have friends right away. She had to see how much God loved her first.

Consider how much God loves you—he created you just as you are and made you to fit right where you are, just like he did for Eve. A friend may not share your love for music. You may feel all alone in pursuing your gifts and talents, but God knows he created you to sing or to play your favorite instrument. A friend might not talk to you on a day she is feeling less than her best. She may be jealous of you. You could take it personally. But God wants you to know how he thinks of you so you don't have to wonder if you fit in. He made you to stand out. He wants you to let your light shine!

There are seven different types of stars in the sky, and they shine differently based on how they are made. They carry different colors depending on their age and life cycle. We are all made differently and have colorful characteristics that make us who we are. God wants you to know that you shine just as you are right now, and he wants you to let others see the beauty you carry so they can recognize God as Creator.

In the same way, let your light shine before others, that they may see your good deeds and glorify your Father in heaven.

Matthew 5:16 NIV

WORDS FOR YOU

You can be yourself with God. He chose you and wants you to know how valuable you are. He created qualities in you that no one else possesses. If you ever wonder how you fit in the world, you can rest assured that you fit perfectly as who God created you to be.

WORDS TO SAY OVER MYSELF

When I don't feel others accept me, I will ask God to help me feel his love, which shines over my life. When I don't know my place with others, I know God is always with me. God brings good things into my life, including friends.

Friends I am praying for:

....

....

....

....

Goals I have to be a better friend:

....

....

....

....

Not Comparing

Starting when we are young, we look at other girls and start to compare ourselves to them. We see the way our friends act or their clothes or even how they look wearing make-up. When we watch them talk with others, sometimes we wonder, "How can I be like her? She's so popular." And when this happens, we think we should be like that person and have their qualities, and our mind starts to question: "Why am I not like her? What is wrong with me?" As these questions worry our minds and settle in our hearts, we start to believe that we don't measure up. We may say to ourselves, "If only I could look or act in such a way to gain friendships like she has," and this starts a cycle of discouraging thoughts.

At the end of the day, all that matters is that you are loved by God and you are made in his image. When we look at others, we pay more attention to them than to our own body, mind, or heart. We give more thought to others than what God intended.

The way to prevent these discouraging thoughts is to fill your brain with good thoughts. Don't compare yourself with other girls. You don't need to be those girls! You were made in a special, unique way. And you can do things in a way that some of those girls aren't able to do.

As you take the challenge to not compare yourself to others, you will notice your life is lighter and the weight to be like others is lifted away.

You can tell yourself, "I am special in how God made me look and the abilities he's given me." Since God chose you when he made you, he knows the kind of good fruit you will bear—the positive choices that will help others see God in your life. And when you ask for anything in his name, he promises to give you what you are asking for when it lines up with who he is. You can be sure that he wants you to walk with confidence as you think over what he would want for your life, not what others say you need. Since he made you, he knows what will make you feel complete, lacking nothing. We are made in God's image and we are so fully loved. Because he loves us, we can place a high value on ourselves. If we don't love who we are, we're going against his decision that we are a good creation. You are his daughter, and he knew who you would be even before your parents welcomed you into their lives. He is an amazing creator who knows in advance what he sees for your life. He holds you close and has his eye on you just like it says in the Bible:

> You did not choose me, but I chose you and appointed you so that you might go and bear fruit—fruit that will last—and so that whatever you ask in my name the Father will give you.
>
> John 15:16 NIV

Acknowledge that the Lord is God!
He made us, and we are his.
We are his people, the sheep of his pasture.

Psalm 100:3

WORDS FOR YOU

Your differences are special because God loves you for who you are. You can help others see who they are, and you can make your own choices without having to look or act like others. You don't have to compare yourself to others and who they are. You can stand firm in cherishing who you are.

My unique gifts:

....

....

....

Choices I can pursue for my life:

....

....

....

How I feel when I make choices that are different from others':

....

....

....

WORDS TO SAY OVER MYSELF

Comparing my life to someone else doesn't help me feel better; it makes me question myself and sometimes feel worse. I know that I don't need to question myself since I contribute something to the world that is different from everyone else around me. I want to focus more on how I stand out in a positive way rather than on what others are like.

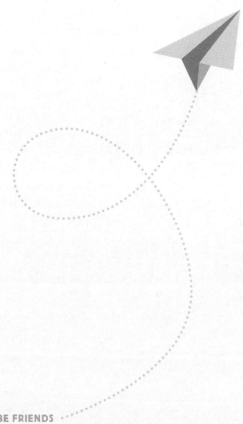

Impressions

When you first meet someone, what is the first thing you do? Do you sway back and forth because you're nervous? Or maybe you look down, because it's awkward to look someone in the eyes and say hello? We all make different impressions without even realizing it.

What do you want your first impression to be when others meet you? If you start at a new school or meet a new person, you want to make a good impression. We might be shy or we might try to make others like us by acting a certain way, even when we know our personality is different. You may try your hardest not to be yourself just so you make a nice or acceptable impression. And as much as you know you should just be yourself, you act differently because you want others to like you. But in reality, you can be yourself! It shouldn't matter what people think of you because you know who you are and you should love who you are.

And who cares if your first impression may not impress others? If it doesn't, then you know you may need to move on and think to yourself, "That person is not for me." You can say, "I don't need to impress her anymore because I have a great personality and I don't mind if people think I'm weird or different." God knows that you are awesome even if you feel awkward in your own ways. Even if it's hard for you to make the first impression you hope to make, when you are who you are on the outside as you are on the inside it gives others the chance to see what makes you who you are!

So the next time you want to impress someone, be true to your personality and not someone else's. The more you act like someone else, the more you're going to dig deeper into the hole of being someone you're not. And once you're in deep, you feel like you can't get out and show others who you truly are.

Solomon was the wisest man who ever lived. He learned about exercising his mind to be smart and filled with the knowledge of God. He wrote the book of Proverbs where we can find a lot of great advice. He reminds us that:

> An honest answer
> is like a kiss of friendship.
>
> Proverbs 24:26

> Walk with the wise and become wise;
> associate with fools and get in trouble.
>
> Proverbs 13:20

WORDS FOR YOU

What you think others may want to see in you may be something they struggle with too. But they want to see something unique in you. Don't be afraid to show the parts of you that aren't the best, and let your bravery help others be genuine in who they are.

What I want others to notice about me:

....

....

....

How can I make a good impression on others?

☐ Listen when a friend is talking

☐ Show respect even if we disagree

☐ Try to end each conversation on a positive note

☐ Ask questions to show that I care about them

☐ Let a friend know that they are loved

WORDS TO SAY OVER MYSELF

I can make a good impression on others even if I haven't done so in the past. I can start now with new and better ways of saying my best words to others. And if I haven't said the best things in the past because I didn't know what to say, I can go back and say to someone: "I didn't really know what to say to you when I first met you. But now that I know you better, I'd like to say _____." I have a chance to try again with someone even if my words didn't go the way I wanted them to before.

Rejection

Some of the hardest days are the ones when you feel that others aren't accepting you. Being rejected never feels good, even if you see that a certain friend isn't the best choice to be around. Rejection never will feel easy. It's a painful, defeating feeling. And the worst part is that girls won't even realize that they hurt you unless they experience rejection themselves. However, it is a part of being in a friendship. Friends will change and friendships will change over time. But God knows the friends who are right for you, and he will help as you call out to him and grow as a person even through rejection. God wouldn't allow rejection if he didn't know that it would help you find the right friends.

He knows it is hard. In fact, God has been rejected by many people. Even his son, Jesus, faced rejection when he lived on earth. A lot of people disobeyed or ignored Jesus, not even realizing how they dishonored him and not seeing the one true God in front of them. Just like you were rejected by your friends, they probably didn't realize what they had done. People may never understand what they have done, and that's hard for us to accept.

But Jesus never gave up on those who met him and denied him, which means he will always love you and find a way for you too. God will turn something that our enemy, Satan, means for harm—rejection—into something that can help you find good friends who will be there for you.

So whenever friends reject you, remember those aren't your real friends and that God will show you your true friends. And that doesn't mean those other friends are mean or bad, they just aren't the friends for you right now; it's time to move on to new friends. God wants you to know that he has set you apart, and you are different from those around you. His Word says:

> You have been set apart as holy to the LORD your God, and he has chosen you from all the nations of the earth to be his own special treasure.
>
> Deuteronomy 14:2

Sometimes being set apart means that we choose friends who value the same things we do, like having a relationship with God, being honest, and being a true friend. Set apart means you stand out, and God sees you as honorable and worthy of having friends who will love you well and love him too.

We want others to like us, and it hurts when they don't show that they approve of us or care about us as much as we care for them. When they haven't invited us to be with them, it can keep us from reaching out to our friends and inviting them to do something with us. Sometimes we want just to know that we are liked, and we will do anything to get someone to like us. But then we can settle and try too hard, when the truth is that we don't have to earn our friends' approval. We should be able to rely on friends, share each other's burdens, and care for each other. When we've been hurt, the easiest thing to do is cut someone off. But God wants us to show love even when it hasn't been shown to us.

WORDS FOR YOU

Even though it hurts to be rejected, God will show you who your real, true friends are, and be with you when it's time for new friends who will support and love you for who you are. Sometimes the best friend for you is waiting on the other side of rejection you have faced.

How can I find new friends?

....

....

....

....

....

....

How will I will treat my old friends?

....

....

....

....

....

....

I will pray for those who have hurt me
rather than speak against them:

Lord, I pray for the friend who spoke words that hurt me. I pray that you would draw her to yourself. I want her to see that you are loving and kind and she doesn't need to use words that put down other people. I pray that you would bring friends into my life who are faithful to you and to me and who would share my values. Most of all, I want to have friendships that are strong and will last, and I ask you to help me see who those friends are. Amen.

Rude Friends
Aren't Worth It

Girls can be kind of rude sometimes, especially when they're going through something. When changes happen, they might treat you rudely, even after knowing you for years. Sometimes it doesn't make sense why friends do this, and if your friend doesn't ever apologize after hurting you several times, maybe the friendship isn't worth your time. Maybe watch how a friend treats your family. Your family is more important than a friendship, so if a friend is rude to your family, it could be time for a new friend.

I (Calyn) had a friendship where one of my friends changed. Based on how she treated me, it wasn't a good friendship for me anymore, so I backed away from her. It was hard, but I noticed how this person made me feel, and it didn't feel good. Soon after, I found one of my closest friends. She chose to spend time with me, and she is one of the best friends I have ever had, and I'm still close with her to this day.

Even though your friends might change and become different, God will never change. He will always be the same mighty God who helps when you ask. He is never rude and he loves you even when you sin. He loves you so much, and he doesn't want you to be with friends who aren't treating you well.

If you ever have a friend or see a person who isn't treating you or people around you kindly, then pray for them. It's hard to know what they're going through, but prayer is very powerful. Even if you don't know how to pray, declaring the name of Jesus over any situation is incredibly powerful. Being kind and nice to them may help them, even when they are changing into someone you may not like anymore.

I have noticed that when one friend's rude actions rub off onto another friend's actions, it gives them the mindset that what their friend is doing is okay. They think they should actually act more like that friend, without seeing how much they are changing as the rude friend showers them with influence. If a person's influence changes you or causes you to question something you've never questioned before, or act in a way that is out of character for you, then it's time to look closer at who you are hanging out with and why. If your friends are all about themselves rather than you, it likely won't be a healthy friendship moving forward. If we are aware of what God says about how we are to act, we'll see the qualities we should carry:

Therefore, as God's chosen people, holy and dearly loved, clothe yourselves with compassion, kindness, humility, gentleness and patience.

Colossians 3:12 NIV

Above all, love each other deeply, because love covers over a multitude of sins.

1 Peter 4:8 NIV

WORDS FOR YOU

God's love for you can help you be kind to others even though they are mean or rude. When girls act rudely, you know that they aren't acting as friends should. But you can still treat them with love as God would want you to. Being kind, even when someone else is acting snobby or prideful, helps you stay true to who you are and want to be. Showing kindness may help others see who they really want to be as well.

Who can I pray for this week, and how will I treat them?

....

....

....

Who are new friends I could branch out to?

....

....

....

Some questions I can ask when finding new friends:

- What are your favorite things to do?
- What do you value more than anything else in your life?
- What are the best traits of a friend to you?
- What are things you like and dislike about friendships?

How someone answers can help you understand her as you start talking and getting to know each other. You can ask God to help you see if this person will be someone that you can expect to have a close friendship with. You can also think of other questions you'd want to know the answer to as you get to know each other.

In any place where we meet others and spend time together, sometimes we need a little time to see if the people around us are friends for us or may be friends for someone else. But sometimes the people we don't think will be a good friend can turn out to be a best friend if we just give them a chance to share who they are.

What Friends Show You About Yourself

Other girls can have a big influence on you each and every day. That's why it's important to find good friends who can help bring out who you are on the inside. How do you find those friends? It's easier than it seems. You want to find those who are different from you and will actually listen to you. The friends who actually want to hear from you, instead of thinking only about themselves, are the ones who can best influence you. Why? Because they care about you and your dilemmas, instead of having an "I don't know" or "You'll be fine" attitude.

And sometimes the friends who don't respect your personality might not last as long as you had hoped, but then you will know that God is saying it's time for a new season and new friends. He knows that sometimes friendships hurt, and it's hard to leave certain friends and make new friends. I wish I (Calyn) could say that all friendships end painlessly, but that wouldn't be the truth. Real friends will help you show who you truly are and wouldn't have you change your personality. It may feel different, but sometimes different is better than "normal" friendships.

Friends can help you realize what you care most about or what you don't really care about. Different friends have shown me more about myself. I can be a little shy or quiet around certain people, but my true friends know this about me and they make me laugh and help me feel comfortable. Instead of making me feel bad about being uncomfortable in certain situations, they show me that it's okay to feel shy.

Sometimes friends may leave your side to be with more "popular" (but kind of mean) girls, and that can hurt. But they will see who the "popular girls" really are as they show their true colors. And when friends compare how they feel around those girls with how they feel around you, you are the one they'll trust because you are kind. You are faithful and strong, even when friends leave you for others, because it's part of who you are on the inside. And you will gain new friends because people see your character and know you are trustworthy.

Therefore encourage one another and build each
other up, just as in fact you are doing.
1 Thessalonians 5:11 NIV

• • • • •

Bear with each other and forgive one another if any of you has
a grievance against someone. Forgive as the Lord forgave you.
Colossians 3:13 NIV

WORDS FOR YOU

When friendships get hard, you can know that you have the opportunity to find who you are in Christ. His truth will help you find who your true friends are. True friends will treat you the way you treat them, with kindness and loyalty. You will learn more about who you are by the friends you're with.

Who are people who are different from me?

....

....

....

Are my current friends actually listening to me?

....

....

....

Would my current friends accept me for who I am?

....

....

....

Learning to Be Confident

onfidence is a trait a lot of girls struggle to have. They want to have confidence, but they are too afraid to really be self-assured. You mainly will see it when you or someone around you is bullied. All of a sudden you lose any confidence you thought you had. You also see a loss of confidence when trying to find new friends, and it's a crushing feeling. But that doesn't mean you can't try to gain your confidence back.

You can start by finding someone you never talk to and ask them a few questions. It doesn't have to be much. And you never know what kind of impact it could have on them. The conversation might seem awkward or uncomfortable, but afterward, it changes you for the better and you find a spark in you that will keep growing. The spark in you is from God, and it can mean that he wants to work through you. He will give you a different perspective on school, friendships, and girls in general. Your confidence will grow only if you decide to make the first move. When you decide to meet new friends, God will help you find and grow in those new friendships. God helps you navigate decisions, but ultimately you are the one who must make the choice to step out.

A lot of times confidence isn't something you get once you have friends. Confidence is what you ask God to give you so that you can find the *right* friends. And asking him to help you have confidence when friends reject you is also important, because it's in those times that you want to lean into God even more so that your identity comes from him, and not from other people.

As you grow more in the identity God gives you, your confidence grows more. One movie in particular, called *The Princess Diaries,* shows a girl who doesn't have much confidence at the start. But as she keeps growing throughout the movie's different situations, she learns confidence and how to stick up for herself against a not-so-good girl. When you grow in ways that include God's values, you find what real confidence looks like. God will show you how to gain your confidence more fully as you ask him to show you if you have a confident mindset or if thoughts of self-doubt are holding you back.

Do not throw away your confidence; it will be richly rewarded.

Hebrews 10:35 NIV

● ◉ ● ● ❚

We can say with confidence, "The LORD is my helper, so I will have no fear. What can mere people do to me?"

Hebrews 13:6

WORDS FOR YOU

You can face the hard things in life if you choose confidence over fear. By choosing confidence, God will reward you with his love and grow the spark of confidence within you.

Who can I talk to that I don't usually talk to?

....

....

....

What impact would it make on them?

....

....

....

How can I build my confidence in inviting new
friends to events, or standing up for myself?

....

....

....

WORDS TO SAY OVER MYSELF

When I lack confidence, I will say to myself, "I am confident in
Christ and I can be confident in my friendships because God
has made me who I am. If others don't accept me, I will keep
my confidence because I know that I'm worth having good
friends. I will keep my eyes open for friends who also show
their confidence in God and don't let their confidence lessen
because of what others do or say to them."

Having the Right Expectations

Have you ever wished for something that didn't happen? Maybe you expected a friend to come support you at your game, or you thought a friend would invite you to her birthday party. We can have expectations of friendships that we thought would bring us happiness, but then wonder if we shouldn't have had expectations of friends who end up disappointing us. Maybe you even say things hoping that others will meet your expectations. But other people rarely respond exactly as we think they will.

We can know what to expect of God, because we learn in the Bible about what he is really like. But many times we put expectations on others that are not realistic. We also need to have the same expectations for ourselves no matter who we are around. If you say certain things and act a certain way toward God, but around your friends you act another way, then something is wrong in your perspective of the importance of God in your life and the level of importance you give to other people. Do you think God won't notice the differences in how you act around different groups of people? I'm not trying to make you feel bad, but I (Calyn) want you to notice how God expects us to act. If those aren't the same expectations your friends might have, you will want to take note of that as you spend time with others. Do they share God's expectations of how we are to act in friendships? What differences do you notice in the different groups of people you are with?

Thinking too much about what others expect can change the way we act. Have you ever thought about how your friendships at school affect how you are using your time at home and how you react or talk to your family? Do you act a certain way just because it's cool, or you learned it from one of the popular girls so you thought it was okay to do it? The way your friends act might not line up with what God says or your own family's values. If you're not sure what the difference is, then pay attention for a few days!

This is not to make you feel guilty or discouraged but I really want you to understand why it is valuable to have the right expectations of yourself and your friends. This is pretty much the only way your friendships and school life can be better. God's will and your attitude toward him matter the most. If you are friends with God first, it will make your friendships with others even stronger.

I can tell you that I was only able to find and keep my new friends because I was strong in my relationship with God and I changed my attitude toward God and friends. You could be friends with anyone, but with God in charge of your friendships, he can bring you unexpected friends who are better for you than you could imagine.

Your attitude can make a big difference in your friendships. What you need from a friend and what you can give to a friend will change as you go through life. Your expectations will change as your friendships change. It is easier to have the right expectations when you are listening to the Holy Spirit and keep a close friendship with God.

The hopes of the godly result in happiness, but the expectations of the wicked come to nothing.

Proverbs 10:28

* * *

The godly can look forward to a reward, while the wicked can expect only judgment.

Proverbs 11:23

WORDS FOR YOU

Your friendships will only get better if you change your attitude toward your family and God, and when you focus on your relationships at home first and then in your circle of friends.

What are some ways I can change my attitude toward God?

....

....

....

....

How will I react better to those who I mistreat?

....

....

....

What should be my expectations of God?

....

....

....

What have been my expectations of friends?

....

....

....

What should be my expectations of friends?

....

....

....

Staying True to Who You Are

S taying true to who you are is honestly pretty hard. Girls tend to try lots of things to get new friends, but I (Calyn) found out early on that my personality and how I treat others is what people care about the most. Also, true friends actually ask how I'm feeling or why I'm acting different if I seem sad or frustrated. I know it may seem impossible to have friends who accept the things that make up who you are, but it happened to me, so that means it can happen for you. When I saw some friends going in a direction I didn't feel comfortable with, I decided not to follow them and started hanging around girls who weren't changing to try to be popular but were comfortable with themselves. They were true to who they were on the inside.

Some people may dislike who you are or what you like, but the truth is some people don't even like themselves, so it's hard for them to approve of anyone. You're blessed to have people who do like you. God has planned the right friends for you, but you may not see what he's doing until you stay true to who you are, rather than trying to change to gain a certain kind of friend. If you have to change who you are to make a friend, they're not a real friend for you. You don't need to base who you are on what someone else thinks of you. God is the only one who can deliver the friends you need because he created you the way you are and can show you other girls who have similar hearts.

Everyone has their own strengths, and that gives a friend group a strong foundation. A friend group will have a weak foundation when everyone is trying to change who they are so other girls will like them better. The strength and trust they could have had in each other doesn't work since they are not being who God created them to be. Staying true means not giving up on what you want in friendships just because other girls are doing anything to try to fit in.

When you make boundaries for yourself, and you have an idea of what happens when you go outside those expectations, then you can see the effects of not staying true to who you are. If you are pretending to be someone you're not, then you are actually lying to yourself, and that makes it harder to trust yourself.

To see who you are underneath everything, you have to ground yourself in the truth. You will begin to believe everything you say about yourself. When your self-talk is negative, you will think of yourself badly. When you lie and tell yourself something that isn't true (like you are bad at something or can't be trusted), you can't stay grounded in who you are. It is totally unnecessary to say mean things about yourself! If you stay true to who and what God says about you, then you will learn not to worry about trying to lie about yourself. You may not always believe good things about yourself, but it shouldn't stop you from saying God's truth over yourself so that one day you may live like it is true.

Since everything God created is good, we should not reject any of it but receive it with thanks.

1 Timothy 4:4

* * * * *

For we are God's masterpiece. He has created us anew in Christ Jesus, so we can do the good things he planned for us long ago.

Ephesians 2:10

* * * * *

Make a tree good and its fruit will be good, or make a tree bad and its fruit will be bad, for a tree is recognized by its fruit... A good man brings good things out of the good stored up in him, and an evil man brings evil things out of the evil stored up in him.

Matthew 12:33, 35 NIV

WORDS FOR YOU

By keeping your identity in Christ, you can know that you bring your own strengths to your friendships, which will bring your friendships closer than you could ever imagine. If your friends don't like who you are, then you can lean on God to help you find the friends who will accept you for who you are.

What strengths can I bring to a friend group?

Who can I turn to if I need help?

....

....

....

How can I live out my strengths with my friends?

....

....

....

How will I stay true to myself in any situation?

....

....

....

Body Confidence

Girls can look at other girls and then look at themselves and think, "I don't look good like her" or "I want to look smaller like my friend." But really, your body is made in a way that God knew would be perfect for the life he has planned for you. Looking at your body and wishing you had a different body can happen as you look around the room at girls your age, or when you are working hard at a sport or dance but still thinking you're not quite right. You might stare at yourself in the mirror and wish you looked different, more like your friend.

But you need to embrace who you are when you see what you see in the mirror. It doesn't matter how other people look (or how they think you should look). You need to believe that your body is made perfectly in God's image, and there's nothing wrong with you or your body. To wish for someone else's body is like telling God, "I don't trust that you made me with your best in mind." Even if you had your best idea of what a perfect body is, it couldn't make you fully happy. But when you trust that God made you gorgeous, you gain a happiness that will stay forever. That joy will provide the confidence to choose truthful, supportive friends.

Since God picked your shape, size, and height, then how does it benefit you to think you aren't worthy of someone liking you? It's easier to criticize ourselves rather than walk confidently in the way that God designed our different features. God sees you as a wonderful creation with no mistakes.

When you repeat to yourself that you are beautiful and you thank God for how he made you, then you will become beautiful in your own eyes. Because we have different ways of being beautiful, we should not look to others to decide how beautiful we are (or wish we were). Comparison doesn't help anyone. Becoming confident in yourself takes time, and we all display beauty in different ways. If someone doesn't like you because of the way you're beautiful, then they are struggling to appreciate how many different kinds of beauty there are. We can't grow in a friendship if we're not feeling confident about ourselves. God wants us to put our hope and confidence in him, because that is where our confidence can never be shaken.

I praise you because I am fearfully and wonderfully made;
your works are wonderful, I know that full well.

Psalm 139:14 NIV

● ◉ • ● ◗

Blessed are those who trust in the LORD
and have made the LORD their hope and confidence.

Jeremiah 17:7

WORDS FOR YOU

When you notice someone else's body, realize they probably have things they would like to change about themselves. You aren't the only one who thinks about her own body. But you are the only one who can control your thoughts about who God made you to be.

WORDS TO SAY OVER MYSELF

I have the body that I'm supposed to have. I don't need to do anything to change my body to be loved any more than I already am. When I'm tempted to think that people accept me because of my body, I will remember that it's what's inside me that draws others to me, not my physical qualities. I want to learn to value my body, but not to let it define who I am.

What I like most about my body:

....

....

....

....

What I will accept about my body that I can't change:

....

....

....

....

....

What I am beginning to see about myself
(even if my friends don't):

_____

_____

_____

_____

_____

Using Words When You Get Hurt

When a friend or person you know hurts you, it feels just like they punched you really hard and it hurts really bad. You freeze and want to break down because you feel so defeated and broken. While it's easy to try and just move on and stuff those broken feelings, using your words to heal those broken feelings is, emotionally, a better way to live through some harder days.

You have to start by being honest with yourself when your feelings are hurt, then be honest with your friends. Don't tell your friends you're fine and avoid telling them how you were really hurt by them. Stuffing your emotions will only keep you frustrated and mad at the friends who caused you pain. I know it might seem awkward or weird to go up to your friends and tell them how you were hurt, but you will be rewarded for doing so. It also doesn't have to be a big ordeal. It can take place at lunch, in the hallway before a class, or before an event you are both attending. It helps to get to the same place in your friendship with each other.

If you don't feel comfortable talking to your friends about

what happened, then maybe you should reconsider your friendship with those girls. Maybe it implies that your friends value your appearance and how you look, rather than who you are on the inside. God sees you as royalty, so he values your emotions and how you feel on the inside. He wants you to be able to use your words to set yourself free from anyone's burdens. He says you can hand any burdens over to him, because he is for you.

I (Calyn) had an incident one day where my friends had hurt me and it made me feel a little disappointed. For about four months, we had all sat with each other every day for lunch, so when one day they did not sit with me with no clear explanation, I was a little sad the rest of the day. When the next day came, I thought hard if I should forgive my friends and ask if they planned to sit with me at lunch. I almost didn't do it, but I knew that it was right to ask them. So that's exactly what I did. I asked one friend about it (who actually had the same thing happen to her, but we didn't know it). I asked another friend, who was really kind and felt bad about what happened, and she said she would make sure we sat together that day. She also said she actually was thinking about me the day before and was feeling bad that she left me. I felt very confident after my talks with both of them, and it gave me a higher level of confidence knowing I can use my words even when I'm hurt.

You can choose if you want to continue to be mad at your friends or forgive them, but if you don't use your voice to communicate, then your pain may grow deeper as you wait and hope they respond to the situation. Sometimes the best thing we can do is to say, "I don't know if you know this, but I care about you." And that can speak to someone in a way that you don't expect. They may look for you to say something mean to them because they didn't act nicely to you. But if we surprise them by saying something kind and true, it can turn them in our direction for the better. If you don't know what to say at the exact moment, you can say that while you are still thinking about the best way to share your words, you want them to know that you don't want to hold onto any bitterness or upset feelings, but want to pray for them in their continued friendships.

I say, love your enemies! Pray for those who persecute you!

Matthew 5:44

● ● ● ● ●

We can say with confidence, "The LORD is my helper so I will have no fear. What can mere people do to me?"

Hebrews 13:6

WORDS FOR YOU

Your words will help you at the lowest and most painful moments. Remember that God uses hard situations to help you have the strength to express to your friends how you actually feel. Even if it seems scary or embarrassing, God will help you out of a hard situation as you step into a weightless friendship without past pain from friends.

How can I use my words to let my
friends know how I'm feeling?

....

....

What words encourage me?

....

....

....

What are words or sayings that discourage me?

....

....

....

How can my words help a friend who is hurting?

....

....

....

Asking Others into Your Friend Group

Nothing hurts more than not being included. Your best friend or group of friends may not have meant to leave you out, but it sure hurts when it happens. When you don't get invited to a party, when you aren't asked to a sleepover, or when you need to choose a partner for something at school and all your friends have already picked partners, those are very hard situations.

It is easy to think, "I wouldn't have had a good time anyway," or, "those aren't my real friends and I don't need to be with them." When we aren't chosen or asked to be a part of something that seems fun, feeling hurt gets mixed up with wanting to protect our hearts from getting hurt again. It can make us want to reject others too, so we try to tell ourselves that we won't allow ourselves to be hurt by the same friends, and we distance ourselves from the people we really want to be with.

In the Bible, there was a woman with an alabaster jar who wanted to see Jesus and went to find him at a very important gathering with the Pharisees. She wasn't invited (because she was known as a woman without a good reputation), but she brought Jesus an expensive gift of perfume and then took the time to show her heart and how much she needed him. The Bible says, "Then she knelt behind him at his feet, weeping. Her tears fell on his feet, and she wiped them off with her hair. Then she kept kissing his feet and putting perfume on them" (Luke 7:38).

Sometimes it isn't about our comfort but how we can serve another friend. Sometimes we need to show up to a friend even when we're not invited. Sometimes not every girl has a friend, so when we show up and are ready to be there for her, it will help her have a sense of belonging. It can give her peace about having a friend she can talk to. My friends and I (Calyn) make it our goal to go up to different girls who seem lonely and start talking to them and welcoming them. You may think this won't mean much to people, but it really does.

When Jesus was at dinner with the Pharisees, they had invited him, but they weren't treating him well. Then someone who wasn't popular came and showed genuine care for Jesus. He was so touched by her sacrifice that he told those who had invited him to dinner: "'I tell you, her sins—and they are many—have been forgiven, so she has shown me much love. But a person who is forgiven little shows only little love.' Then Jesus said to the woman, 'Your sins are forgiven'" (Luke 7:47-48).

If Jesus forgives sinners, we can forgive our friends. We can also ask others to join our friend group and show them their worth. When we do the right thing of including others, it can help us overcome our sad feelings when we aren't included.

No one likes to be left out. It makes us feel like others don't see us. But Jesus sees us. He saw the woman who anointed his feet, and He sees you and me.

*At the resurrection of the righteous, God will reward
you for inviting those who could not repay you.*

Luke 14:14

* * *

Wisdom is shown to be right by the lives of those who follow it.

Luke 7:35

WORDS FOR YOU

Even if you haven't been included when you really wanted to be, you can invite others to join you and your friends. Know that God would want you to help others feel like they are invited. You can show love to others even when you sometimes feel left out. God would want you to forgive others just like he has forgiven you. Be a friend who helps others feel like someone is looking out for them!

*Dear friends, let us love another, for love comes from God.
Everyone who loves has been born of God and knows God.*

1 John 4:7 NIV

What girls do I know who need comfort?

....

....

....

....

How can I make them feel welcome, like
Jesus welcomed the woman?

....

....

....

WORDS TO SAY OVER MYSELF

I don't have to wait for others to invite me into their friend group. I can make the choice to go ahead and bless others before they invite me in. I can ask them to join me where I am developing friendships. I can praise God for the friends I do have and share with him when I feel a lack of friends in my life. Admitting the lack I feel can keep me coming to God and depending on him to satisfy my heart and to bring friends who will have the same values.

I praise you, God, in the overflow of friends and in the lack I may feel at times. Thank you for helping me see how you are moving in my life at all times even when I don't see it. I trust you will bring me just the right friends who will help me grow into the person you have called me to be.

Earning Trust

We talk a lot about trust in these devotions because that's how you become a good friend. This is honestly pretty hard to talk about because trust is usually not permanent. But that does not mean you shouldn't ever trust others, because then no one would want to be your friend. Why wouldn't they be your friend? The first way to gain a friend is by building a trust connection. What that means is that friendships are made stronger when you trust each other, and are both trustworthy. If you keep lying (which goes back to our devotion of "Staying True to Who You Are"), then it is harder to be a good friend.

God is trustworthy, so when we choose to trust him, it's one way we display ourselves as Christians. When other people lie to us, we lose trust, but we know that we can trust anything God says. Even though friends might lie to us, we should give them a chance at earning our trust. Some people lie to get more attention, just like the enemy uses lies to try to get your attention and influence you to choose the wrong response. But as followers of God, we should never lie to others.

Trust is something that you develop over your entire life.

You can develop trust with others by first building trust with God, who is always more trustworthy than your friends. Learning to trust your friends is a constant process that takes time. There are times when they will lose your trust, but if you choose to trust them again then it will teach them that they do not have to lie to you. But if they are continuing to lie and deceive you then you know they are someone you should not trust or invest in as a friend. In other words, don't try and trust in a friend who is continually lying to you. And don't spend too much time trying to earn their trust, because they have proven they aren't trustworthy.

As you build trust with friends, it helps you see which girls are following God. Sometimes "popular" girls, who seem like they wouldn't lie, are disguising their lies behind a smile to try to make themselves look better to their friends.

We will always be working on earning and offering trust, but it if we keep trusting in God during tough situations then it won't be as painful because we know what real trust looks like. When we start up a conversation or invite someone to do something together, it builds trust. The other person sees that you see something inside of them that you think is worthy of friendship. You earn trust when you are able to offer your friendship and time with them.

A gossip goes around telling secrets, but those who are trustworthy can keep a confidence.

Proverbs 11:13

This is what the LORD says: "Cursed are those who put their trust in mere humans, who rely on human strength and turn their hearts away from the LORD."

Jeremiah 17:5

WORDS FOR YOU

You can show your trust in God before others as you walk in truth and not lies. He will show you what truth looks like, and you will show others how you walk in truth and sincerity. Trustworthy friends bring you comfort when you need it, and you can lead others to the comfort and safety they need from God.

In what situations do I need to trust God right now?

....

....

....

How will I walk in God's truth?

....

....

....

In what situations has my trust decreased?

....

....

....

Who are the girls in my life I can trust?

....

....

....

....

....

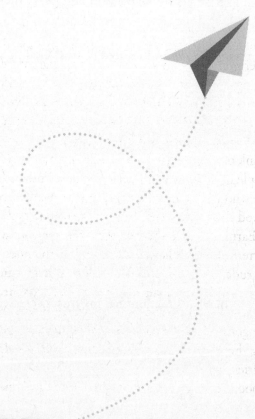

Good and
Not-So-Good Friends

I f you have ever seen girls gossip or say rude things about other girls, and you know that it's wrong, but it keeps happening, those are not good friends to have. But if you've seen girls encourage and treat other girls with kindness, then those are the good friends to have. But have you ever felt like it's hard to tell between them sometimes?

Think of some characteristics that resemble God, and think of people in your life who you know have those characteristics. People who don't have those characteristics are people who are not good friends to have. Kind of like we learned in our devotion "Earning Trust," the people who display kind and loving characteristics are followers of God, but the ones who gossip or say rude things about others—or to others—are not God's followers. Although some people say they are Christians, they may not actually be pursuing God, which means they still may not be good friends. And sometimes Christians get lost in following their not-so-good friends, but you can help them find good friends again.

Good friends want to stick by your side and encourage you,

because they genuinely enjoy being with you. Not-so-good friends won't spend much time with you because they are still learning how to value others. If you don't feel encouraged in a friendship, then you know that person isn't a good friend right now. You will want to make more time for good friends who value your well-being and enjoy having you with them. Girls can struggle to find friends because girls can change year to year, and sometimes your best friend in one grade may not be your friend in another. It can be frustrating, and you don't really know what to do about it, but remember that good friends continue to value their time with you.

The quality of a friend is more important than how many friends you have. So, signing up for a friend who is not trying to follow God is definitely not worth it (even though it's tempting to gain more friends). You are capable of many things, like taking time to find caring friends, but forcing friendship with girls who aren't ready to be a good friend doesn't help you. You don't need to rush God's timing when it comes to friendship; ask him to help you wait for good friends. If you're trying to find friends on your own without God's assistance, then how would you know if they're good friends? People can lie. You have a whole lifetime of friendships ahead of you, and it's wise to ask God to help you navigate through your friendships.

A good person produces good things from the treasury of a good heart, and an evil person produces evil things from the treasury of an evil heart. What you say flows from what is in your heart.

Luke 6:45

Turn away from evil and do good. Search
for peace, and work to maintain it.

1 Peter 3:11

WORDS FOR YOU

With God's help, you can find good friends even in hard times. Knowing his good character traits will help you know what good friends should look like. Good friends help you instead of working against you. God will also know who are good friends for you to have and who will be there for you.

There are "friends" who destroy each other, but
a real friend sticks closer than a brother.

Proverbs 18:24

Who are girls I want to become friends with?

....

....

....

Would they actually care about me as a friend?

....

....

....

Who in my life resembles God?

....

....

....

Which of my friends could make me
stronger instead of weaker?

....

....

....

How to Find Good Friends

A fter reading the devotion "Good and Not-So-Good Friends" and seeing the differences between those types of people, now let's look at how to find those friends who would be best for you.

For starters, you have to think of your dream friend—the kind of friend you really want to have in life. Kind of like shopping—you think of the item that you want (or in this case, the friend you want) and what qualities stand out to you. When you're shopping, you go through all the options until you find the one that fits you best. With people it's a little different, but you can start to see which friends "fit" you as you watch how girls treat other girls and look at their priorities. You can also try and talk to them. This can take a while, because everyone is different and every person will have qualities you like but also qualities you may find odd.

If you want to narrow down good friends faster, then look at how they treat you. Set your limits on how you want to be treated—just like how you set a budget when you're shopping. Never push the limits (even though you might do it when you're shopping). It's not a good idea to push limits in your friendships; a good friend wouldn't want to push limits or try to take advantage of you. Although it may take some seeking and observing, you can really start growing in a friendship by just talking to those who are nice and treat you well.

Finding those friends could take a lot longer than expected and may be challenging. In the end, finding good friends in your life is worth all the rejection and all the hard moments—just like after you climb a mountain you can see something incredible and all the hard moments fade from your memory. Good friends are so worth it in the end. Plus, you never know the impact you can have on them. I (Calyn) was actually able to lead some of my best friends to Christ, and they are now helping others do that as well. Finding good friends is like finding who you are in Christ. You know where you belong and why. It can be confusing and girls will betray you, but when you find those who are actually good to you it can really warm your heart and it makes you even more grateful.

When you have a great friend, you can find your passion for things you never thought you would enjoy. You may find out why God wouldn't let you have those other friends. You will know deep inside that no one could ever do what the good friends in your life are doing for you. You will trust God more on the path he is leading you on because he knows what's best for you. Friends are important people in our life, so take your time finding the good friends. The wrong ones will only hurt you.

The seeds of good deeds become a tree of life; a wise person wins friends.

Proverbs 11:30

We can make our plans, but the Lord determines our steps.

Proverbs 16:9

WORDS FOR YOU

You will find good friends when you look for qualities that God approves. It might take time, but it will be worth it in the end. Good friends will come at the right time, and you can find the best ones by seeing how they treat you and others.

Who are the girls who treat me well?

....

....

....

Who are the girls I think I could be friends with?

....

....

....

Would God approve of those friends?

....

....

....

Am I ready to find friends?

....

....

....

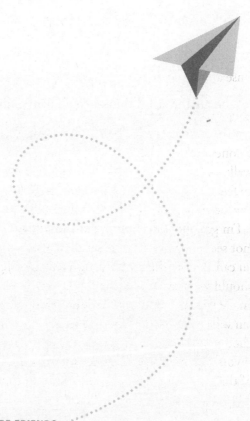

When to Walk Away

I t can be hard to make friends, so we usually want to hold on tight to the friends we have. But sometimes you may realize a friend is not actually very good for you. If you realize you feel tense around someone or don't feel your best when you are with them, and you've already tried to talk with them about how they make you feel, it may be time to walk away from that friend. You are the one to decide when you walk because you are the one making boundaries with your friends. And how do you walk away? How you should walk away is also up to you. It may feel easier to just abandon your friend, but it's better if you can be honest and talk to them. Even just saying, "Hey there, I'm going to go sit with another friend at lunch so you may not see me as much" is better than just disappearing.

You can't ignore the problem. You will need to decide when you should walk away because if you stay with those friends who make you feel tense and anxious, it will keep hurting you. You can walk away at any time you feel uncomfortable or don't feel good about a situation. You can tell them how you feel, and if you don't know what to say, there are some ideas at the end of this devotion. If your friends have a problem with you wanting to walk away or how you express your words, that may show that they weren't meant to be your friends anyway.

It's hard to stand up for yourself, especially if your friends don't like that you're walking away or think that you are being hurtful to them. Sometimes the truth will hurt, and not everyone likes to hear it. You don't have to feel guilty. You are smart to walk away from friends who have "disapproval" for you, or who want to make decisions for you, or who are not respecting what you want versus what they want for you.

We can walk away confidently from those not-so-good friends. Friends won't always like what you are doing, and it is really easy for them to tell you things to make you stay when you just want to walk away. You want to be graceful about it, but you can stand up to them and say, "This doesn't feel right to me." You shouldn't have a friend always telling you what to do.

Remember, you get to set the boundaries for your friendships. If you are being pressured to leave certain friends because someone else doesn't like them, or if you are having peer pressure to be with people you don't like, then maybe the one pressuring you is the one to walk away from.

Walking away from friends can give you a chance to branch out more and be with people outside of those friends. We can walk away feeling better when we know it was the right decision, and when we trust God to bring us better friends.

Then you will understand what is right, just, and fair,
and you will find the right way to go.

Proverbs 2:9

So follow the steps of the good, and stay
on the paths of the righteous.

Proverbs 2:20

WORDS FOR YOU

You can walk away from friends when you have uncertainty or don't feel your best around them. You should never feel stuck with your friends. Being with friends should not feel like a chore; it is supposed to be uplifting, special, and helpful.

Ways to walk away from your friends:

- Give them reasons why they have been great friends, and then share why the friendship is hard now, and that you think it may be time for some space.

- Tell them it may be better if you find some new friends because sometimes you don't like how they act toward you, or because of a quality about your friendship that is hard.

- Be honest about your feelings, and understand that they may feel differently.

- Give examples of how they helped you in a season of life, and share how you think it is time to find a new friend to help you in a different season.

- If they want you to stay in the friendship after you share your feelings, but they are not changing their behavior, then hold your ground. Be honest about how they are hurting you, that you don't like it, and that you want friends who will treat you better.

Am I more comfortable telling a friend how I feel and leaving, or not telling them how I feel and staying with them?

....

....

....

....

Do I have friends I would rather be with?

....

....

What types of qualities do they have?

....

....

....

....

Would I feel confident walking away, or do I need more time to prepare myself for what I may face?

....

....

....

Honoring Others Who Are Different from You

We all have traits and opinions that set us apart from others; those are our differences. Although we don't always like a person's differences, we know it is right to honor them in such a way that shows respect. Sometimes we're not sure how, but here are some ideas.

When you are put into a group project and you are trying to figure out what you are doing and everybody is shouting out ideas, instead of disagreeing and thinking how some ideas may not be what you wanted, try to share what you think (in a kind way). You can share how you could make it better while still honoring what others think. You bring your different ideas together with their ideas, so you can both be honored. Or when you see how someone dresses very differently than you, instead of treating them abnormally, be kind and spread the love of God to them. God has made each of us with certain interests and tastes, and you can honor someone by giving them the same respect and kindness that you wish to receive from them.

I (Calyn) know you don't always want to honor others,

especially those who maybe have hurt you or you just mainly dislike, but God will help you do it. As hard as it is, we too can honor those who are different. When we honor others, we show God's goodness, as he honors us when we choose him. One of my mentors, Tiffany, says honor means, "If it matters to you, it matters to me."

God rewards those who honor his wonderful creations and it will impact others when you do so. When we honor others it will open doors to new heights. It can vary for each of us because God is leading us on our own paths, but I can tell you that giving people respect and kindness will make the path even better for you. Throughout your life, you will actually spend a lot of time honoring many people, so it would be wise to start now when you're younger so you don't have to figure it out later. There will be people you come across in life who you will have a tough time honoring, but it will get easier as you keep learning the true meaning of why we honor, which is to show others that they are important and matter to us and to God.

Our differences might feel really sharp when we first meet others, but as we spend time with them we will come to understand them better, and we'll be able to honor our differences in ways that we wouldn't see if we just avoided certain people. Differing qualities and interests make any relationship more special, and when we honor that diversity it can make our friendships stronger. When you honor the unique things you see in a person, you could end up being best friends with someone you might not have picked at first. That's how you can branch out to new friends.

There may be girls who wish they were different, born into a different family, or who aren't sure who they really are. They may be confused about the way God made them. You can choose to love them even if they question God or if they aren't sure of how loving God helps them in their friendships. You can show them genuine love. Even if you don't have a lot in common, you don't agree on everything, and you don't see life the way they do, they are still people you can love. As Jesus loved all sorts of people, we are to love others and show them the reason for our love, which is his sacrificial love for us.

Love each other with genuine affection, and take delight in honoring each other.

Romans 12:10

Don't let evil conquer you, but conquer evil by doing good.

Romans 12:21

WORDS FOR YOU

You can honor those who are different from you. As you do, you will learn to honor God and notice how he treats his followers and creation. By honoring people and their differences, you can grow in how you see people around you, and this will show you how good God actually is.

Who do I have a hard time honoring?

Would God honor them?

....

....

....

How can I honor them?

....

....

....

Would my kindness help them to be more kind as well?

....

....

Not Gossiping About Others

When we talk with our friends, they might start a conversation about how they don't like another girl's clothing or hair. And you might be thinking, "Oh, well that wasn't very nice," but they say, "Oh no, it's okay because she won't know we said that. And if she asks, we'll tell her it looks great." But that right there is *gossiping* (and lying) and there are many things wrong with gossip.

For starters, the friends who gossip are girls who do not act like very good friends. Girls who gossip don't seem to know how to talk about others positively—it's almost always negative. Second, it really is rude to talk about girls behind their back! You should not be telling girls one thing to their face and saying another behind their back.

Gossiping is destructive. You may think you don't gossip, but you could be doing it without knowing it. Many people don't want to admit they've been talking behind someone's back or not telling the whole truth. Someone could be lying to you about someone else, and you might not know it, because if confronted, most people will deny they said anything bad about someone else. If you just say whatever you hear others say (even out of sympathy or wanting to protect someone else), you could be restating a lie that brings someone else a lot of pain. It's better not to repeat anything you hear when it comes from gossip.

But you don't have to be stuck in gossip, and here's how you can keep from gossiping about others. When a girl starts talking about another and it starts out as something like, "I don't like her," or, "I think she would look better if," then you instantly know you need to get out of this conversation. It should make you feel angry that someone is gossiping about another girl. After all, how would you feel if they talked about you like that? God can give you the confidence to speak up and tell those girls that it's wrong. Don't let a lack of confidence hold you back from getting out of gossiping and getting into conversations that honor each other instead.

You can also back away from gossiping by saying positive things about a girl. For example, if one girl says, "I don't like her new hair," then you can say back, "Well, I really love her new shoes and I think she looks good with her hair like that." That will make the other person wish they hadn't said anything and they probably won't want to say anything else. When you shut down those conversations, you're basically shutting down any darkness trying to speak through those girls, and the power of God will show up in that moment to make room for light in your friendships.

Let these false prophets tell their dreams, but let my true messengers proclaim my every word.

Jeremiah 23:28

● ◉ ● ● ◗

*Then you will again see the difference between the righteous and
the wicked, between those who serve God and those who do not.*

Malachi 3:18

●●●●●

*You, dear children, are from God and have overcome them,
because the one who is in you is greater than the one who is
in the world. They are from the world and therefore speak
from the viewpoint of the world, and the world listens to them.
We are from God, and whoever knows God listens to us; but
whoever is not from God does not listen to us. This is how we
recognize the Spirit of truth and the spirit of falsehood.*

1 John 4:4-6 NIV

WORDS FOR YOU

Talk positively about others! You can be kind and compliment girls whenever you see them. When you bring positive and uplifting words into a conversation, you can overturn any gossip, and it will keep you from gossiping too. You will also help other girls stop gossiping. Remember that if they continue to gossip, they may be struggling with their own life or making themselves the center of a friendship, and with this behavior they are also hurting themselves.

Are any of my friends gossiping? How could I stop them?

What type of words should I use to stop from gossiping?

....

....

....

Am I getting trapped into gossiping? If
so, how can I help myself not gossip?

....

....

....

Can I stand up for myself and tell those girls
why gossiping is bad or negative?

....

....

....

Letting Friends See Your Weaknesses

When you don't feel the best about something you said or did, you may have a hard time letting friends see your weaknesses. You may do everything you can to not let someone notice that you are feeling down or sad. When you think you have not done as well as you could have, or you have something that you can improve on in your life, something inside of you starts to come to the surface, but deep down your sadness or disappointment could be felt as frustration.

All of us have weaknesses we try to hide. But when we try to hide, we aren't being genuine with ourselves or our friends. We want the kind of friends who will love us for who we are, not for how we do in a skill, in a sport, on a homework assignment, or in any area that's not our strength.

What is hard for us to realize is that when we let others see our weakness, it helps them see that we aren't perfect, which actually makes a friendship stronger. You may not even realize if people see you as such a strong person that they assume they don't have anything in common with you. Some people won't approach you to be friends or talk with you if they think that you don't have any weaknesses.

Of course, you don't want to make up a weakness just to try to fit in. But when you can share with a friend something you struggle with, it helps them connect with you better. They realize that you may even have some of the same weaknesses they do. Others can better relate to you when you are real and when you let them see how you live your life.

One of the ways you can be real about your weakness is to say, "Did you know I struggle with _____? Have you ever struggled with that?"

And if you don't do as well on a math test because math is harder for you, and when you have disappointment written on your face over a homework assignment or test, share this with a friend, even if they did well. You can say, "Math isn't my best subject, but I try. I have other subjects I like and do better with. Some subjects are harder for me and, when I'm feeling weak, that really bothers me and changes how I see myself. Sometimes I don't think I'm that smart, but rather than let the situation take over, I need to believe in myself more."

You can turn a weakness into a strength when you go from thinking negatively about yourself to just realizing that everyone has different things they're good at, and that's okay. When you are open with others, they see that you are honest and not boastful and that it's okay that you aren't good at everything. No one likes to be around that person who always brags on themselves and doesn't show any weaknesses.

How would God want you to show others your weakness? How can you embrace that as part of your unique identity?

That's why I take pleasure in my weaknesses, and in the insults, hardships, persecutions, and troubles that I suffer for Christ. For when I am weak, then I am strong.

2 Corinthians 12:10

WORDS FOR YOU

Commit to being honest before God, and being open with your friends as well. When you see a weakness, recognize that it's an area in which you can grow. Learning from your weaknesses helps position you to be a better friend and a more humble follower of Christ. True friends accept you for your strengths and your weaknesses.

Sometimes you may feel a weakness is a reason to stay away from your friends. But your friends have their weaknesses too. You need to stand up for yourself if a friend puts you down for a weakness, or doesn't know you the way God knows you or the way you know yourself. It's okay for you to be honest about how you see your strengths and weaknesses. Weakness doesn't mean you're a less valuable person or friend!

Weaknesses are not limiting to who I am, but they can limit what I do. What weaknesses would I like to overcome?

....

....

....

WORDS TO SAY OVER MYSELF

Being humble is different from being weak. I will ask God to help me with any area of my life that becomes a weakness. I don't have to view myself as weak in my friendships. And I won't let my friends' choices affect mine. I am strong in my thoughts, choices, and actions and I can reflect what I know God wants me to do. I can pray a prayer asking God to help show me who I am so that others can see how our imperfections help us live unguarded with friends:

God, it's not easy to admit that I am weak in an area, or more than one area, in my life. But I know you can use my weakness to help others see that no one is perfect. Help me not to stay down on myself for any weakness, but to look for ways I can show your strength in me and in others. Amen.

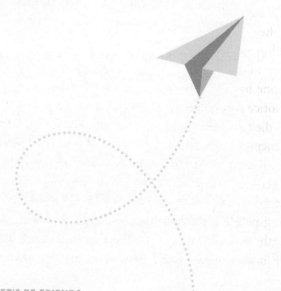

Sharing the Strengths You See in Others

Do you like it when a friend tells you they like something about you? It helps you feel better about yourself, doesn't it?

Just as it's important to let others see your weaknesses, you can help your friends see their strengths. When you tell others the strengths you see in them, it boosts their confidence. And they remember and appreciate you for giving them a compliment.

You might not think that just noticing a strength that someone has could really be that helpful. But maybe the day you notice and point out a strength to a friend could be a day when they are feeling sad or disappointed. Your comment can help them see that a friend knows how great they really are.

We like to think that we offer a unique strength. We feel stronger—as individuals and with our friends—when we help someone else feel truly seen. It may be that you are great at making people feel comfortable around you. Or you have a strength for making conversation, especially in situations where it can be awkward. Maybe others tell you that you know just what to say to make them feel better. Your strength could be in the way you care for people by listening. If a friend needs to talk, you don't always need to say anything right away. Sometimes people just need to know you care, and maybe later you'll think of what you can do to help your friends.

When you offer admiration, it shows that you aren't afraid to shine the light on someone else. It's admirable to share something kind about other people, even if they don't offer a compliment to you. When friends see that you notice a strength in them, it shows them that you have paid attention to them and your friendship. You win friends when they see that you don't have to be the one who takes the spotlight or is always on top.

Continue to love your friends, even when it's not easy to accept everything they do or say. As you encourage them and love them, you will see God's love shine through you.

Encourage each other and build each other up, just as you are already doing.

1 Thessalonians 5:11

* * * * *

Dear friends, since God so loved us, we also ought to love one another. No one has ever seen God; but if we love one another, God lives in us and his love is made complete in us.

1 John 4:11-12 NIV

WORDS FOR YOU

One way you can be a good friend is to point out a strength you see in someone else. You can look for genuine ways to point out to others their positive characteristics. We all like to know that someone sees something in us that they feel is meaningful. You can seek to find at least one way to compliment your friends, especially when you see that they can use some encouragement.

I see these strengths in my friends:

....

....

....

....

....

WORDS TO SAY OVER MYSELF

When I point out strengths I see in my friend, I notice that she feels grateful that I'm willing to lift her up. Noticing her strengths helps me keep my eyes off of just myself and focus on my friends. I feel like a better friend when I can do this.

I would like to be known for these strengths:

....

....

....

....

I can be honest and say that I would like for my friends to notice me too. But if they don't, I can remember the strengths that God has given me. I believe that some of the strengths I have help me in my friendships. And I'm going to pray for new strengths that I can take into my friendships in the future.

God, I want to be a friend who notices others' strengths, but also lives out my own. Will you show me what you consider to be the gifts you've put inside of me? I want to live out of the strong and courageous places you have created inside of me, and I ask you to help me see them and not be afraid to go for it as I live my life in front of my friends. Amen.

Why It's Important to Have a Relationship with God

When you go to church or read your Bible, you might notice the Bible talks a lot about a relationship with God and what it will look like. But why do we have this relationship established between you and God?

He is like your friend who knows you better than anyone else, and he will never leave you. He will always help in challenging and impossible situations where there seems to be no way forward. God doesn't fail you like some friends do, and he can be your safe place to turn to when everything feels hard. It is more difficult to figure out your purpose and path in life without God because he knows you best, and he knows the best way to help you handle your struggles. No one will ever love you more than God. As you spend time building your relationship with God, you will see how God can help in all of your relationships, even with friends who are not Christians and may want to influence you to go another way.

It can be hard to be with God when sin—an action or thought that isn't Christ-like—is surrounding us. Other people's influence can break us down, but when we choose to be with God, his influence can be stronger than anyone else's influence. There will be times when you have to trust God and his timing, but the waiting will one day make sense and you will see how well his timing works.

Our relationship with God is so important because his power is greater than the lies the enemy tells you.

In 1 John 1:5-7, the Bible talks about how God is the light. There can be times when we think we are living in the light, but we are actually making choices that cause us to live in darkness. There is no darkness in God, so it can be hard for us to see him when our choices don't honor him. But when we live in the light, we see God more clearly because God is all light. He will forgive us from all the sin that tries to drown us.

We find that in our hardest moments, when we don't feel like we can do it anymore, God will help because he loves us so much and doesn't let his children suffer alone. It's important to be in a relationship with God because he can help you with your friendships. He wants to give you the kind of friends and situations in life that will help draw you closer to him. Choosing to live without God ultimately hurts you, because no one can comfort you like God does.

This is the message we heard from Jesus and now declare to you: God is light, and there is no darkness in him at all. So we are lying if we say we have fellowship with God but go on living in spiritual darkness; we are not practicing truth. But if we are living in light, as God is in the light then we have fellowship with each other, and the blood of Jesus, his Son, cleanses us from all sin.

1 John 1:5-7

*You must worship no other gods, for the LORD, whose very name
is Jealous, is a God who is jealous about his relationship with you.*

Exodus 34:14

WORDS FOR YOU

When you get into a relationship with God, then you can
know that you'll have comfort, love, support, and a God
who never lets you down. Others will see that you're stronger
because God gives you strength. With God, know that you can
overcome anything and will be stronger in your faith when you
believe him.

How can I make my relationship with God strong?

....

....

What are some challenges that God can help me with?

....

....

How will I stay in my relationship with God?

....

....

Why do I need to trust God right now?

....

....

How can I ask God to help me with a
problem I need fixed right now?

....

....

....

....

....

Building a Foundation of Faith

My mom bought me a Bible that had illustrations in certain sections. I (Blythe) loved looking at the pictures because I wanted to picture what Jesus looked like. My foundation of faith was reading that Bible. We didn't have cell phones back then, but we carried around our Bibles. I remember thinking as a child, "When do we stop going to church?" I'd see older teens who were past high school and still going to church. Soon I realized that going to church and reading my Bible was a foundation you never outgrow. We don't ever "stop" reading God's Word and learning from him.

Have you ever made a great cookie recipe that you just loved? Do you remember the foundation for it? It probably had some main ingredients like flour, butter, and sugar, but then you added in some other ingredients to make it really awesome. Your foundation is what helped the cookies to rise. Baking powder is good for that! The Holy Spirit is what helps us rise in our faith because the Holy Spirit's role is to be our comforter, counselor, and helper when it comes to our faith.

Some people think the Holy Spirit is something you feel

(or don't feel), but God's Word tells us that the Holy Spirit is one with the Father (God) and Son (Jesus). Isn't that cool to think about? When we read the Bible, the Holy Spirit convicts us—in a good way—of what God is saying to us. The Holy Spirit can comfort you when you are having a hard day or have lost a best friend. The Holy Spirit can guide you when you are unsure of what to say to a friend, and the Holy Spirit can help you to choose the right recipe of friendship for your life.

When you gather the ingredients for your cookie recipe, you know you need all the ingredients working together to make the cookies as delicious as you want them to be. That's how your faith is. Faith is in every part of your life, and you build a foundation of faith when you read your Bible, when you talk with God, and when you sense what he's speaking straight to your heart. He loves you so much!

When someone tastes something delicious and says, "How'd you make this?" they are recognizing that you created something really special. When others see that you have the ingredients in your life for a life that is tasteful to the Lord—and to them—you know that you've built a good foundation of faith. You get to decide how important it is for you to believe and trust God in your life and your friendships. Whether you realize it or not, right now you are laying a foundation for your life. What do you want your foundation to look like?

In this way they will lay up treasure for themselves as a firm foundation for the coming age, so that they may take hold of the life that is truly life.

1 Timothy 6:19 NIV

WORDS FOR YOU

You are building a foundation each day, from the time you wake up to the time you go to sleep. What you think about, what you focus on, and what you spend time on will either build your foundation of faith in God, or you may start to see cracks in your foundation. Each decision you make can either strengthen or weaken your foundation. You can start over by building a strong foundation for God so that you can say, "No matter what my friendships with others look like, my friendship with God is strong. He is the one who holds me up."

You can first lay a strong foundation with God through prayer. Make sure you're praying to God not just for your friends, but pray to be someone who seeks him more than anything else in your life. Create a pattern of prayer in your life so that you know you're talking to God and listening to what he wants to say to you.

A prayer I can pray:

....

....

....

....

WORDS TO SAY OVER MYSELF

I will also lay a foundation with God through reading the Bible. I know I can get answers to issues I face and encouragement I need when I read his Word. I will keep my heart open and ready to hear what God has for me. His words will equip me for each day of my life.

I know there's no perfect recipe for creating a foundation of faith. And I know it's not my actions that draw God to me, but he draws close to me because of his love. So I will make my best choices and build time into my day to be with God so that I can hear his voice above all others. I can build something beautiful in my life when it is based on God.

Favorite verses I have read:

Staying Present in Your Faith

Do you ever look back on an event in your life and realize you've been thinking too much about how you responded? Or do you ever think over and over about how you should respond to something a friend does or says? It can be easy to stay overly focused on either the past or the future. We can have our attention pulled in a lot of directions. So how do we stay present in our faith and not give up or get distracted?

Queen Esther, whose story is in the book of Esther in the Bible, became queen after going through the preparations needed to be ready to meet the king. When a close confidant to the king, Haman, wanted to attack the people of her Jewish faith, she was willing to risk her life to protect their freedom by speaking up for those she loved and respected.

In those days, even though she was queen, she still had to make a special request if she wanted to meet with the king, and she knew that if he didn't like what she had to say, that could be the end for her.

She went before the king, her husband, who had the power

to grant or deny her request. She met with him more than once before she made her big request. When Esther told the king that their enemy, Haman, was calling for her people to all be killed, the king was filled with anger. Haman had meant to end the lives of all of Esther's people, but instead the king responded by ending Haman's life. Esther's people's faith was rewarded, and Esther's courage won their redemption from the hateful act of a powerful man. She definitely stayed present in her faith, she didn't give up, and her reputation stood firm as she was honored for speaking up. She was persistent and present to the needs around her.

Do you notice how when you spend time with God you are able to pinpoint areas around you where you can make a difference? Friendships that last will require faith to keep them going. Because there will be days where we don't feel like we're making a difference or that our friends don't like us as much as we hope. We need to rely on our faith rather than on what a friend thinks of us or what they might say in a tough time.

In Esther's time, Haman was an enemy because of his pride, jealousy, and desire to have what wasn't his. You might be around friends who act that way at times. The best thing for you to do is to remain faithful to what God has called you to and to be a voice to others of what is right and good. Just like Esther, you have the ability to protect those you love and stand up for your faith.

If a friend makes fun of your faith or tells you that only weak people need God, you can share with your friend that actually it's strong people who realize that if God wasn't in their life they wouldn't be able to do all that God has called them to do, which is pretty big! The opportunities and recognition that God gives us are more fulfilling, and we don't have to hurt people to get ahead or use people to get what we want (like some people do).

You are called to lead people just as Esther did so that others can know God and his deep love for them. When we stay present in our faith, we don't allow others to pull us in the wrong direction. We can get distracted by so many voices we hear through texts, chats, social media, or in the halls or the lunchroom, that we don't pause to listen deeper for what God wants to say to us. Spending time with God by reading his words in the Bible helps us know exactly what our focus should be.

Esther risked her life so that others would have life. Through her boldness, God's people were saved. Jesus did the same thing for us. He was willing to give up his life so that we may live.

> For even the Son of Man came not to be served but to serve others and to give his life as a ransom for many.
> Mark 10:45

WORDS FOR YOU

Be someone who speaks up on behalf of others so that they have the full life that God offers us all. You may risk your reputation or what others think of you when you speak up for God, but it will be worth it. God will take care of you like he did for Esther and her people. Don't be afraid to speak the name of God to your friends, but remember it is his name that will free them from every fear, worry, or problem they face.

How can I stay present in my faith?
(Check the ones you want to try.)

- ☐ Daily prayer time with God
- ☐ Reading God's Word daily so I can identify truth
- ☐ Asking God to deliver me out of a situation that's hard, like Esther did
- ☐ Looking for God's power and miracles around me

WORDS TO SAY OVER MYSELF

Being purposeful in my faith and in my relationship with God is how I'm going to get through some of the hardest days of my life, especially with how friends can change. When God is the one who is constant in my life, I'll be able to understand how my relationship with him doesn't change even when my relationships with others do.

Where is God calling me to lead and
how do I know it's his calling?

....

....

....

What are the type of friends who won't
distract me from my calling?

....

....

....

Taking Your Pain to God

When someone you have been friends with mistreats you, betrays you, or hurts you with her words, deep pain can set in. You can feel sick to your stomach or feel nervous or even dread seeing or hearing from the person who caused you to feel unnoticed or left out. It can really rob you of the joy and the life that God came to earth to give us.

God is the only one who can take away your pain. He sent his son Jesus to take on all our pain so that we would have hope for the future and be forgiven of all the wrongs in our lives.

Instead of feeling sorry for ourselves, we can honestly tell God how we feel. "God, this hurts. I didn't see this coming. I feel taken advantage of, used, and discarded. I know that whether my friend meant to hurt me or not, you are the only one who can help heal my heart. Will you show me what's true about who I am?"

It's hard to separate ourselves from the truth of who we are and the reality of what happens to us. We aren't deserving of someone's intentions to hurt us. Sometimes we'll never know why someone does something to hurt us.

You may be thinking that everything is going well with your friend and then all of a sudden you are surprised to hear they've been talking bad about you, or they send you a hurtful message, or you stop hearing anything from them at all. And then you realize that your friend is no longer friends with you, but is friends with another friend of yours, and you learn that they are hanging out together and you haven't been included.

It also hurts to know that someone may have only wanted your friendship to get to someone else. It makes you wonder if you can trust that person in the future or if you can trust any of your friends.

Sometimes we want to get back at the person, even just a little bit. We know it is wrong, but on the inside we want them to feel what we feel—rejected. In times like this, we need to pay attention to our emotions. We might be sad, angry, frustrated, disappointed, or betrayed. We need to be able to tell God, "This is the emotion I'm feeling. I know you don't want me to stay in a place of hurt. With your help, I'm choosing not to think about this situation over and over, and instead think of how I can help someone who maybe needs a friend right now, just like me."

There's an encouraging verse that says God will take care of us and the person who hurt us. Even though it's tempting, we aren't to take revenge. We can trust that God will deal with them as he deals with us when we need to be corrected. He says:

> Do all that you can to live in peace with everyone.
> Dear friends, never take revenge. Leave that to the
> righteous anger of God. For the Scriptures say, "I will
> take revenge; I will pay them back," says the LORD.
>
> Romans 12:18-19

If a friend has used you to get what they want, chances are they have done the same thing to someone else before you. It doesn't take away the pain you experience, but it does help when we know that it's probably not the first time this has happened. It might help you to consider whether that person was really a good friend for you.

When you experience hurt for the first time, it's good to remember that you can learn how you don't like to be treated and how you don't want to treat a friend. If a friend hurts you often, you may want to think about how this person's actions can rub off on you and what you may do to others without even recognizing it. When that happens, it is probably time to walk away from your friend who is repeatedly hurting you or not being a great influence. You can refer back to the devotion on "When to Walk Away" to think about the best way to talk with your friend. If you're not able to talk safely, send a message to them expressing your heart in a loving but firm way.

When you take a stand for yourself and talk about how valuable your heart (and their heart) is and that you don't want to compromise, you can leave the door open for the person if they choose to change how they handle your friendship. But until then, remember that God has called you to a different path when you line up your heart with his. His path for friendship is based on loving values and respect for others.

On the next page is a quick check for your heart in this season. If you relate to the emotion listed, there's a good verse for you to remember.

- "I feel angry."

"Don't sin by letting anger control you." Don't let the sun go down while you are still angry, for anger gives a foothold to the enemy.

Ephesians 4:26-27

- "I feel lonely."

He Himself has said, "I will never desert you, nor will I ever abandon you." So that we confidently say, "The Lord is my helper; I will not be afraid; what will man do to me?"

Hebrews 13:5-6 NASB

- "I feel disappointed."

Do not fear, for I am with you; do not be dismayed, for I am your God. I will strengthen you and help you; I will uphold you with my righteous right hand."

Isaiah 41:10 NIV

May you remember that pain is not meant to stay in your heart to make you feel bad or teach you a lesson, but it is an invitation to go deeper into the heart of God.

WORDS FOR YOU

You can take all your emotions to God—even your past frustrations—and trust him to care for you in a way that no one else can. He sees what is happening in your life and he is the one who will help you feel better when no one else understands. Even the most hurtful pain can't defeat the love God has for you.

How am I inviting God to come into my pain?

....

....

....

Why am I still holding onto pain when
God wants me to let it go?

....

....

....

Becoming Part of God's Family

If you have never accepted God into your life, or if you aren't sure if you have, then this devotion can help you find your place in God's family. I (Calyn) want to share some conversation ideas you can have with God as well.

If you want to become part of God's family, then the first step is to learn more about him and what he is about. Reading the Scriptures is a great way to get to know God. You will read about how he is creative, how he heals people, how he saves his followers, and why he needs to be the only God in your life. Committing your life to God is a big decision. You want to get to know someone before you commit your life to them, so you don't have to rush. When you are ready, God is ready, and then you can commit a prayer to God, repenting of your sins and asking to be part of his kingdom.*

This can be hard for some people because not everyone has had a good life. Your past might make it seem unbelievable that you could be born into a new life and have a new start. It's

---

* Check out page 137 for more on how to do this.

okay if you have a hard time believing God has made you new, but God will help you in your new season. God is more than excited to be close with you now. He is celebrating with you!

It doesn't matter what age you are because God accepts anyone into his family. Everyone is invited to be in a relationship with him. When you decide to become part of his kingdom, you will meet people you wouldn't have otherwise known. You will also get to keep learning about God and growing in your relationship as he takes you along the path he made for you. Even when you think God isn't with you, the Bible tells us he's there and he can help you with any unbelief. God will show you just how excellent his works are, and as he brings you through tough situations, you'll grow closer with him in the end. It is also super cool to have God as your heavenly Father who loves you unconditionally!

After you decide to be with God, he will give you callings and challenges, which will help you have a deeper understanding of how good God is. Once you become a follower of Christ, you can help others do the same and help them know God. You can invite them to church or tell them about the Bible and some of the stories from it that stand out to you. God will direct you on how to help others. You may have a path in life that is different from others because God gave us all special gifts to display and show others.

Remember, becoming part of the family of God is not exclusive whatsoever—anyone who believes in God can join his family. He wants us to follow him for the rest of our lives so that we don't have to go through life separated from him. It's God's desire that all men and women would follow him, but it's up to our individual choice to do so.

The Lord...is patient with you, not wanting anyone to perish, but everyone to come to repentance.

2 Peter 3:9 NIV

We love each other because he loved us first. If someone says, "I love God," but hates a fellow believer, that person is a liar; for if we don't love people we can see, how can we love God, whom we cannot see? And he has given us this command: Those who love God must also love their fellow believers.

1 John 4:19-21

Here are some conversations you can have with God about being a part of his kingdom:

- Dear God, thank you for your everlasting love. I pray that I can have new life in you with my heart set on your kingdom for the rest of my life.

- Dear God, I pray that you would restore what was broken in my life. I give you my hopes. I ask for your blessings in Jesus's name, and I thank you that I can live freely in your kingdom.

- Dear God, I pray that I can be made new in your kingdom and that you would forgive my past sins. Thank you for your grace and goodness and that you give me new life and a chance to help others.

- Dear God, thank you for what you have shown me in the Bible. I pray that I will now live with you, God, and that I can be free from any sins and trouble that may make me pull away from you. God, I want to be with you and model to others how good you are.

WORDS FOR YOU

When you're ready, you can become part of God's family. As you get to know God, you can relate to him as your heavenly Father. He will help whenever you need it, and he will give you gifts and talents to help others know about him. As you follow him, he will give you what you ask from him that is in step with who he is, in his perfect timing.

How will I get to know God?

....

....

....

How can I find time in my day to study God's Word?

....

....

....

Who is supporting me in my relationship with God?

....

....

....

How can I express my gifts or talents for God?

....

....

....

Who around me needs to hear how to be in God's family?

....

....

....

Am I ready to hear from God and step
into a new season of life?

....

....

....

Thinking on God's Word

We have talked about how important it is to read God's Word, the Bible. But in the Bible, we actually learn that we're supposed to meditate or think on the words that God shares with us. Meditate means to think about something (a lot!) and let it play in your mind as you try to live it out.

Meditating on God's Word isn't some practice where you have to be in a certain mindset or be super-spiritual. It just means that you spend time thinking about what God says, maybe even more than what your friends say.

We hear a lot from our friends, but God wants to say even more to us. He wants our attention, our affection, and even our very best efforts to love him and show others who he is in a world that often doesn't understand what God is really like. Our relationships—and others' understanding of God—can really start to change for the better if we and our friends spend time reading what God says about himself in the Bible and share what he has shown us after reading his Word.

That's really what it's all about. You can't get to know a friend if you don't spend time with them, right? We get to know what God's heart is when we spend time with him. Sometimes people don't understand how reading the Bible can really help you. But even if you spend five minutes of reading the Bible instead of five minutes just entertaining yourself, you will see the difference it makes. A funny video doesn't transform your life, but the Bible does. Joshua fought against people who didn't respect him and didn't like him, yet God told him these words: "Study this Book of Instruction continually. Meditate on it day and night so you will be sure to obey everything written in it. Only then will you prosper and succeed in all you do" (Joshua 1:8).

And Joshua did succeed by listening to what God instructed him to do, and he conquered territory that God made ready for him. God does this for us, too, when we meditate on his words and obey what we read.

Do you have a favorite Bible story or favorite part of the Bible? You could start there by reading and meditating on a verse a week, and then try to grow into more than one verse a week so you are expanding what you are learning.

If you haven't read the book of John in the New Testament, it is a really helpful place to start. This book shares what it means and looks like to live as a believer in Christ. It has some very wise things to say to us.

Where are you drawn to meditate on God's Word? Is there a Psalm you really like? There's a lot of encouragement for us in that book of the Bible. The Bible is full of actual events and stories that draw us into the wonder of living with God, here on earth, and in heaven one day.

WORDS FOR YOU

Words can stand out to you when you read the Bible. If you meditate on God's Word, God will show you truth, and he will help you change for the better. You can grow in wisdom and be encouraged as you read the Bible.

Oh, how I love your instructions! I think about them all day long. Your commands make me wiser than my enemies, for they are my constant guide. Yes, I have more insight than my teachers, for I am always thinking of your laws.

Psalm 119:97-99

What does this verse mean to me?

How does God help me have even more insight, now and as I grow, when I think about what his Word says?

And now, dear brothers and sisters, one final thing. Fix your thoughts on what is true, and honorable, and right, and pure, and lovely, and admirable. Think about things that are excellent and worthy of praise.

Philippians 4:8

Spend time meditating on Philippians 4:8.
Which words stand out to you?

....

....

....

What would you like to think about more and what
would you like to think about less so you're focusing
on what is honorable, admirable, and true?

....

....

....

What are steps you can take to transform your thoughts
when they aren't going in a good direction?

....

....

....

Write a prayer to ask God to help you fix
your thoughts on the right things:

....

....

....

Journaling with God

Journaling in a notebook and writing down your thoughts is a great way to be honest with yourself and express how you feel. You can also do it with God in the same way when you write down your thoughts to him. When you share your thoughts on paper, it will show how you're honestly dealing with things and what you may be struggling with. It can also be fun to design your journal with different colors and express your thoughts in a way that is unique to you.

You can start journaling with God by grabbing some paper and a pen and just starting to write about any problems you have—things that seem really hard. I (Calyn) used to journal about some hard challenges I faced and how it made me stronger. You could journal about how God is moving in your life and what he has already done to help you. It's fun to also write down some verses that have some meaning to you, and you can make them look fun with different colors or different styles of writing.

After you have written in your journal you can look back and watch how much you have grown in the years and see how faithful God is to you. God will help us when we show him how we feel. And if we are struggling with different areas of our life, that's okay because God knows everything about us and even how to help us. Journaling will help get your thoughts out of your head so they don't put an unnecessary weight on you. Some of your negative thoughts are lies, and writing them down can help you understand where these thoughts are coming from.

There was a man in the Bible named Joseph who was betrayed by his brothers and sent to Egypt to be a slave. He kept trusting God, and he was eventually delivered out of slavery. We have that story because someone wrote it down for us so we can see how good God is when we trust in him. Another man in the Bible was Paul. He kept getting sent to jail for telling people about Jesus, but he would write a ton of encouraging letters to the people he loved and these letters ended up becoming a big part of the Bible.

When it is hard to juggle the situations in your life, God can help you. As you write in your journal, God already knows what's hard for you, but journaling is like a quiet time to reflect on how things are in your life. It's taking a step back and thinking on ways God can help you and what you can pray to God about.

As for me, I look to the LORD for help. I wait confidently for God to save me, and my God will certainly hear me.

Micah 7:7

So we keep on praying for you, asking our God to enable you to live a life worthy of his call. May he give you the power to accomplish all the good things your faith prompts you to do.

2 Thessalonians 1:11

WORDS FOR YOU

When you journal with God it will help you express your feelings to him so you can know how he will help you. When you meditate on what you write, believing for something better, you will be blessed in God's perfect timing, and you can gain the confidence and power to keep growing and pursuing him now.

What are some journaling ideas I want to talk to God about?

....

....

....

What verses can help me keep trusting God?

....

....

....

How can I keep pursuing and growing in God?

....

....

....

God wants us to be honest. He can handle even our most difficult thoughts. Our enemy, Satan, wants to distract us and cause us to doubt that God is there for us. But we need to remember that when we come close to God, he is already there for us.

Humble yourselves before God. Resist the devil, and he will flee from you. Come close to God, and God will come close to you.

James 4:7-8

Pressing On When Life Is Hard

Some days are just harder to get up and get going. Have you ever noticed in movies how they switch to slow motion during an action scene or when the filmmaker really wants you to notice something in detail?

Our God is like that too. Sometimes he slows us down so that we can take in what he wants us to see. What is your favorite image? Do you like the beach? The mountains? The forest? The art studio? Maybe it's even a shopping trip! So many possibilities!

What do you love most about your favorite image? Is it how it makes you feel? No matter how many times you go to those places, it becomes a place in your mind that is worth going to, right?

When you think about the places you love, it can help you press on during the days when life is hard. Knowing you have a place that cheers you up can be exactly what you need.

Maybe even picture what you love to do in those spaces. Read, write, listen to music, take a walk, tune out the world.

It's okay to even tune out your family for a little while and think about what decisions you need to make, how you will get through some hard circumstances, and what you want your life to look like on the other side. Sometimes we'll think, "I want to be really good at _____ and have my friends notice how hard I've worked," and that helps us press on when life is hard in a subject, sport, or activity.

Other times we say, "I want to be a good friend and have these friends for a long time in my life." The choices we make to shape our character and to be a good friend help us press on when life is hard.

Sometimes friendships can help us through the hard times but sometimes friends don't know how to respond to us when we're walking through a hard time. People often don't know what to say because they haven't experienced exactly what we're walking through. We don't want to hold it against them if they don't say the right thing.

Pressing on when life is hard doesn't mean you have to fake being happy or pretend that everything is all right. Pressing on means that you decide what you are going to focus on and what you are going to do next in your life. Going back often isn't an option (or at least it's not a good option). How will you be different as you press on?

Sometimes you will have a different sparkle in your eye even when you've gone through something really hard. And other times you might cry more often, and that's okay too. You are doing what you need to do in order to press on. If you can share with a trusted adult how you need their support, I bet they would love to be there to talk with you and help you as you think about the future. You are so worth having someone invest in your life, whether it's a parent, grandparent, or friend.

You are wise to ask for help when you don't feel like you can do everything on your own.

Then Jesus said, "Come to me, all of you who are weary and carry heavy burdens, and I will give you rest. Take my yoke upon you. Let me teach you, because I am humble and gentle at heart, and you will find rest for your souls. For my yoke is easy to bear, and the burden I give you is light."

Matthew 11:28-30

WORDS FOR YOU

You can be honest with yourself and with God when you're struggling. Being honest means admitting that you're not able to carry everything on your own and asking God what you're supposed to give over to him. Spending a lot of time worrying about or fearing the future is not going to help you keep going toward what God is doing in your life. But talking to God and asking him to help you see what he has for you is how you'll keep moving forward.

In what areas of my life do I need to press on and press into God more?

....

....

....

....

....

How can I ask my friends to encourage
me when I go through hard times?

....

....

....

....

....

How can I trust God to help me know what friends will
be there for me in the good and hard seasons of life?

....

....

....

....

....

You're a Warrior

an you name a great warrior you look up to? Real or fiction. She wasn't really a warrior but she was my favorite: Wonder Woman. I (Blythe) loved to see her fly into action. One minute she was living a real, ordinary life. And then wham! She turned into Wonder Woman with a cape and she jumped into action.

There are many warriors in the Bible, but one who actually helped write the Bible is David. That's right—he was a warrior and a king, but he also wrote many of the songs in the book of Psalms.

But I bet he didn't always feel like a warrior. He was out working in the fields as a shepherd when the leader Samuel directed David's father, Jesse, to bring him in. Samuel was the prophet sent to anoint the one who God chose to be king.

> But the LORD said to Samuel, "Do not consider his appearance or his height, for I have rejected him. The LORD does not look at the things man looks at. Man looks at the outward appearance, but the LORD looks at the heart."
>
> 1 Samuel 16:7 NIV

Jesse had David brought to Samuel, and the Lord said, "Rise and anoint him; this is the one" (1 Samuel 16:12 NIV). After he was anointed as king, David had times where he made bad decisions. But he always came back to God and poured out his heart. He recognized what he did was not right in God's eyes. David led many battles, but I think the biggest one that he won was turning to God when he messed up.

God knew ahead of time that David would mess up. Yet he still chose him. One of the psalms says,

> Long ago you spoke in a vision to your faithful people.
> You said, "I have raised up a warrior. I have selected
> him from the common people to be king."
>
> Psalm 89:19

And God chooses you too. No matter what you have done, he still chooses YOU!

How does God raise up a warrior in you? Through your obedience, when you honor his name and don't use his name inappropriately, and through your dedication to him above other things that pull at you—these honorable decisions turn you into a warrior for him. But we have to learn to put God above the influences of others, what friends have or may be doing, or any action or thought that takes you away from your focus on him.

How do you remain a warrior? Warriors take a stand. That's what some of our favorite heroes do. How? Read this:

Stand your ground, putting on the belt of truth and the body armor of God's righteousness. For shoes, put on the peace that comes from the Good News so that you will be fully prepared. In addition to all of these, hold up the shield of faith to stop the fiery arrows of the devil. Put on salvation as your helmet, and take the sword of the Spirit, which is the word of God.

Ephesians 6:14-17

WORDS OF WARRIORS

- I am strong as a believer in Christ even when I feel hopeless or weak.
- I am loyal to God even when I don't understand him or what is happening in my life.
- My heart follows God even when others don't.
- God prepares me for when I face a battle.
- I have my integrity of character that yields to God.
- I will rise to the challenges before me.
- God has called me to action and I will finish what I start.

What do I do when I feel less than a warrior?

What qualities do I have that I can use when I face any battle?

....

....

....

....

....

Longing for God for a Lifetime

Do you long for a special occasion, like your birthday? Do you finish one birthday only to start planning your next one? A lot of us look forward to a certain holiday and we plan for it and count the days until it comes. Sometimes we even say, "I've been waiting my whole life for this."

Have you ever looked at your relationship with God that way? That you are so excited to journey with him, to see what you and he can do together? That you are focused on what he's doing in your life and you can't wait to see the plans he has for your life?

We (Calyn and Blythe) think longing for God for a lifetime is a great desire to have. He is, after all, the very best friend you could follow.

What do you dream of? Do you have things you want to do, either by yourself or with your friends? A camping trip, a trip to the beach, starting a new hobby? Feeling like you have a future with the friends you dream of having?

There's longing in each of us. Longing for something more. And God is the very best friend who can check the boxes for what we want to happen in our lifetime. In the Bible, the prophet Jeremiah recognized what God was up to, saying this: "Long ago the LORD said to Israel: 'I have loved you, my people, with an everlasting love. With unfailing love I have drawn you to myself" (Jeremiah 31:3).

Friends go with you along part of your journey. And sometimes they take a different path as you both grow into the places God has for you to travel. It can be hard to let go of some of your friendships. And we lean heavily on God to help heal our hearts when that happens. Remembering that God has drawn you to him helps you not feel lonely or forgotten.

Friends help us through many things we go through in life. Good friends listen, they care about you, and they want the best for you. Sometimes friends leave us sooner than we want them to. But God will never leave us.

We long for God the way we long for security, friends, and acceptance in our lives. But he gives us a reason to want to follow him for a lifetime. The way we can go through all that we go through is because God holds us. He is like a blanket of love around us. When the warmth in our friendships fade or we feel like our friendships have lost the flicker of light that keeps them going, God tells us that we are to look to him to know the truth of how we are loved and how we can love others. Because his love in us is complete, we can love others out of his love.

Dear friends, since God so loved us, we also ought to love one another. No one has ever seen God; but if we love one another, God lives in us and his love is made complete in us.

1 John 4:11-12 NIV

Longing for God looks like making time for him even when it doesn't feel convenient or as desirable as connecting with a friend or going out to eat or buying something new. But when you make time for God, he fills you up and even gives you something extra to share with your friends. When you look at your relationship with God over a lifetime, you will look back and see how he gave you what you could pass onto others—genuine love and acceptance.

- You can replace your longing for a friend's acceptance with a friendship with God who has loved you ever since he created you.

- When you make room for God in your life, he affirms you in every way you need him to.

- Longing for God will not disappoint you because God is always faithful.

- Letting your friends know that they can also create a relationship with God that lasts a lifetime is a great way to invest in your friends.

- When you love your friends selflessly, God gives you everything you need to keep loving them.

I have told you these things so that you will be filled with my joy. Yes, your joy will overflow! This is my commandment: Love each other in the same way I have loved you. There is no greater love than to lay down one's life for one's friends. You are my friends if you do what I command.

John 15:11-14

I can pray a prayer of blessing over my friendships:

God, I want friends who will accept me and love me but also love you. I want friends who honor you and consider you when they make decisions in life. I want to pray protection over my heart that I would seek more and deeper friendships that reflect your love. You created all of us to have friends and to love others and treat others well—even if they don't always treat us the way we want to be treated. But I know I'm to look for friendships that put you above anyone else and don't compromise values that you say are good, true, and right. I make a commitment this day to come to you when I'm not sure about a friend, and I commit to ask you to help me when a friend turns the other way and my heart hurts from their actions or words. Thank you for always being loyal to me and showing me what a faithful God, creator, and friend you are and always will be. Amen.

Signed

Date

Friends with Jesus

Dear Friend,

We want you to see what the gospel of Jesus Christ is all about and be able to share this message with your friends.

Jesus is the son of God who came to earth over 2,000 years ago and lived as a man. We learn about him in the Gospels (Matthew, Mark, Luke, and John)—the first four books in the New Testament section of the Bible. You should check it out!

"The gospel" just means the "good news" of how Jesus came to take away our sins. Long ago, in the Old Testament, the prophet Isaiah explained how Israel and all nations could be saved from our sins:

The people who walk in darkness will see a great light.
For those who live in a land of deep darkness, a light will shine.
...For a child is born to us, a son is given to us.
The government will rest on his shoulders.
And he will be called: Wonderful Counselor, Mighty God,
Everlasting Father, Prince of Peace.
His government and its peace will never end.
He will rule with fairness and justice from the
throne of his ancestor David for all eternity.

Isaiah 9:2, 6-7

Jesus is the son who the father God sent to us, and he gave his life for us. Adam and Eve were the first man and woman, and they disobeyed God (Genesis 3:6). We follow in their footsteps because we are descendants of Adam. We are all sinners: we all sometimes choose our own way instead of God's way. We will have moments where we sin and don't even realize it. Romans 3:23 says, "For all have sinned and fall short of the glory of God" (NIV). This verse tells of how when we sin it is hard to feel like we are part of God's kingdom, but the good news is that Jesus died on a cross for our sins so we can be redeemed. He will take away our sins if we are willing to ask for his forgiveness. He doesn't want our past experiences to stop us from being in his kingdom.

God's Word tells us, "For the wages of sin is death, but the gift of God is eternal life in Christ Jesus our Lord" (Romans 6:23 NIV). We can be so consumed in our sins that we don't accept what good God can do for us. When you join the kingdom of God, you feel a supernatural presence that even in hard days he is still there for you.

One verse we keep holding onto is 1 Peter 4:19 which says, "So if you are suffering in a manner that pleases God, keep on doing what is right, and trust your lives to the God who created you, for he will never fail you." God can sometimes put you in places you think may be bad for you and you would want to leave, but when you trust God in those situations, something good will flourish from it.

If you believe in Jesus and believe in the promises he has, then you are ready to be in God's family. Romans 10:9 says "If you declare with your mouth, 'Jesus is Lord,' and believe in your heart that God raised him from the dead, you will be saved" (NIV).

Matthew 6:33 says that we are to "Seek the Kingdom of

God above all else, and live righteously, and he will give you everything you need." That includes living forever with him in heaven!

We talked about the family of God in the devotional titled, "Becoming Part of God's Family." This is so exciting, because even if you don't have a family you feel close to right now, you get to be a part of God's family.

In Ephesians 1:5, it says, "God decided in advance to adopt us into his own family by bringing us to himself through Jesus Christ. This is what he wanted to do, and it gave him great pleasure." God chose you from the very beginning. He wanted you—more than you will ever know. God's ready with open arms whenever you are ready to choose him too.

Having a relationship with Jesus is important to having good friendships. He shows us how to be a good friend and he helps us love friends through his power. He gives us the strength to keep making good choices even if others don't.

How do you have a relationship with Christ? You simply pray a prayer like this:

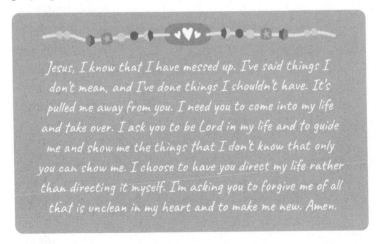

Jesus, I know that I have messed up. I've said things I don't mean, and I've done things I shouldn't have. It's pulled me away from you. I need you to come into my life and take over. I ask you to be Lord in my life and to guide me and show me the things that I don't know that only you can show me. I choose to have you direct my life rather than directing it myself. I'm asking you to forgive me of all that is unclean in my heart and to make me new. Amen.

It's really helpful to remember that Jesus will never betray you. But when a friend betrays you, it becomes an opportunity to become more Christ-like. We learn to forgive just as Jesus Christ has forgiven us. Sometimes we get offended because of pride in our heart. That's when we want to ask God to forgive our pride or anger and help us to be clean on the inside, getting rid of these ugly thoughts, feelings, or actions. He promises to do that in 1 John 1:9: "If we confess our sins, he is faithful and just and will forgive us our sins and purify us from all unrighteousness" (NIV).

We are so thankful that you have taken this journey with us and we welcome you into the family of God!

Calyn and Blythe

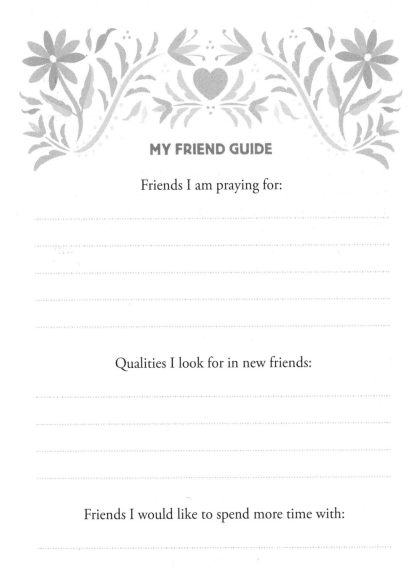

MY FRIEND GUIDE

Friends I am praying for:

....

....

....

....

....

Qualities I look for in new friends:

....

....

....

....

Friends I would like to spend more time with:

....

....

....

....

....

What I've learned about my friendships:

....
....
....
....
....

What is hard for me about trusting new friends:

....
....
....
....
....
....

What I appreciate about my current and past friends:

....
....
....
....
....
....

WORDS WITH FRIENDS

Let your friends write messages to you here!

What my friends say about me that I'd like to remember

From: ....

Things I appreciate about you:

....

....

....

....

From: ....

Things I want you to know:

....

....

....

....

From: ....

Things I see in you:

....

....

....

....

From: ....

When I think of you, I think...

....

....

....

....

From: ....

Things I admire about you:

....

....

....

....

From: ....

Ways I have grown by knowing you:

....

....

....

....

From: ....

....

....

....

....

From: ....

....

....

....

....

RECIPES FOR FUN

When friends get together, sometimes you like to create things you can either eat, wear, or use! Here are some ideas you can make with your friends, or you can make them for your friends and surprise them with a treat! You can vary the recipes and even do a bake sale or have a party using these and other recipes you create together!

STRAWBERRY BANANA SMOOTHIE

Ingredients

    1 to 1½ cups milk (any kind of milk is fine)
    1 to 2 cups frozen strawberries
    1 banana
    1 scoop protein powder (use your favorite!)
    1 T. turbinado sugar (optional)

Directions

Place all of your ingredients into a blender. Blend until everything is fully mixed and looks smooth. Pour it into cups for you and a friend to enjoy. You can double the recipe to make more!

Serves 2

CALYN'S CHOCOLATE CHIP COOKIES

Ingredients

   1 cup salted butter, softened or melted (if you use unsalted
      butter, add a pinch of salt to the recipe)
   ¼ cup sugar
   ¾ cup brown sugar
   2 eggs
   1 (1.4 oz.) package sugar free vanilla pudding (secret
      ingredient!)
   1 tsp. vanilla extract
   2¼ cups flour
   1 tsp. baking soda
   2 cups semi-sweet chocolate chips

Directions

Preheat the oven to 350°. In a large bowl, combine the butter
with both sugars and stir until they are fully mixed. Add your
eggs one at a time until each is mixed in. The batter should
start to be getting thicker. Stir in the pudding mix and vanilla
until everything is well combined. Then mix together the flour
and baking soda, and add this to the batter. Once you have a
doughlike consistency and there is no flour visible, add your
chocolate chips. Scoop the dough into evenly-sized mounds
and space them evenly apart on a cookie sheet, about 12 to a
sheet. Bake for 8 to 10 minutes and look for browning edges to
indicate they are ready to come out. Once the cookies are out
of the oven, immediately take them off the baking sheets and
put them in a single layer on cooling racks or a plate.

Makes 18 to 24 cookies

STRAWBERRY YOGURT PIE

Ingredients

16 oz. strawberry Greek yogurt
16 oz. Cool Whip, thawed
2 tsp. lemon zest
2 cups fresh diced strawberries
1 store-bought graham cracker crust

Directions

In a mixing bowl or large bowl add the yogurt, Cool Whip, and lemon zest. Stir well. Stir in the cut strawberries. Pour the mixture into the crust, scraping in every last bit of filling. Cover the pie with clear plastic wrap and freeze it overnight, or for at least 4 hours. To serve, you can add more Cool Whip, whipped cream, or strawberries.

Serves 8, or slice it smaller to serve a larger party

CHOCOLATE PIE

This recipe makes enough for 2 pies.

Ingredients

    1 cup semi-sweet chocolate chips
    2 sticks (16 T.) butter, melted
    4 eggs
    1 cup sugar
    1 cup shredded coconut (optional)
    2 frozen pie shells in tins, regular size, not deep-crust

Directions

Preheat the oven to 350°. In a microwave-safe bowl, melt the chocolate chips and butter. Blend in the eggs, sugar, and coconut (optional), and pour the mixture into the 2 frozen pie shells. Bake the pies together for approximately 35 minutes. The top of the pies will appear crusty and you can put a toothpick in the pie and see if it comes out clean to indicate it's ready.

Each pie serves 10 with slightly smaller than normal slices
It's very rich-tasting!

CHERRY CHEESE TARTS

Ingredients

24 vanilla wafer cookies
16 oz. cream cheese (2 8-oz. bars), softened
¾ cups sugar
2 eggs
1 T. lemon juice
1 tsp. vanilla
1 (21 oz.) can cherry pie filling

Directions

Preheat the oven to 350°. Place 24 foil cup liners into the wells of two standard-size muffin tins. Put one vanilla wafer cookie in the bottom of each cup.

Cream together all remaining ingredients except the pie filling. Pour the batter into the muffin cups, filling them halfway. Bake the tarts for 15 minutes, then cool them on wire racks. Remove the foil liners from the tarts. Set the tarts on a plate. Put 3 cherries and a small spoonful of sauce on top of each tart and either refrigerate or serve them right away.

Makes 24 tarts

MY FRIENDS HAVE TAUGHT ME THESE RECIPES:

CREATING MEMORIES AND MEANINGFUL MOMENTS

Two people are better off than one, for they can help each other succeed. If one person falls, the other can reach out and help. But someone who falls alone is in real trouble.

Ecclesiastes 4:9-10

Creating with my friends helps me to remember…

....

....

....

....

....

Crafts I can make with or for my friends include…

PROJECT:	TO MAKE FOR:
☐ Candles with a friend's favorite scent	....
☐ Christmas tree ornaments with our photo	....
☐ Handmade greeting cards, notecards, and special occasion cards	....
☐ Bible verse cards	....

PROJECT:	TO MAKE FOR:

☐ Friendship bracelet with a friend's favorite colors ....

☐ Luggage tag ....

☐ Decorative bags with colorful drawings for gift-giving ....

☐ Bookmarks ....

☐ Magnets for lockers ....

☐ Paint a mug with a Scripture verse ....

☐ Sketch book with places I have been and drawings or encouraging notes ....

☐ Key chain ....

☐ Decorative photo board ....

☐ Paint a canvas of a friend's favorite item ....

Friends' birthdays to remember:

....

....

....

....

....

Friends taught me to do these things that I enjoy:

....

....

....

....

....

....

My favorite gifts that friends have given me:

....

....

....

....

....

....

QUESTIONS
I CAN ASK MY FRIENDS

Sometimes you might not know what to say when you're talking with a friend or don't feel like you have anything to say. Maybe you can't think of anything new to ask a friend. So here are a few ideas for you to use or say in your own way:

- What is something new you are doing these days?
- What are you enjoying this year in school compared to last year?
- How are you feeling about the changes you're going through?
- Do you feel like you have support from me right now?
- What do you value most about being my friend?
- What are you looking forward to as you move into the next grade?
- Is it hard when your sibling wants to do the same thing as you?
- How are you doing with not having any classes or activities with friends?
- What is a goal you have this year?
- What do you do when you feel lonely?
- What is your favorite hobby that you didn't think you'd like but you do?
- What is something I don't know about you that you'd like me to know?
- What makes it hard for you to trust a friend?

- What hurts you the most in a friendship?
- How do you like to celebrate your birthday?
- What is your favorite way to spend time with a friend?
- Why do you think we are such good friends?
- How can I pray for you?
- What do you like most about having friends?
- What would you like to do if you could go anywhere in the world?

WORDS FOR YOU

Even when your friends have things that you don't have, remember not to worry about what you have now or what you'll have in the future. When you seek him first, there's no end to what God will give to you and show you about friendships and his plans for you.

Therefore I tell you, do not worry about your life, what you will eat or drink; or about your body, what you will wear. Is not life more than food, and the body more than clothes? Look at the birds of the air; they do not sow or reap or store away in barns, and yet your heavenly Father feeds them. Are you not much more valuable than they? Can any one of you by worrying add a single hour to your life?

And why do you worry about clothes? See how the flowers of the field grow. They do not labor or spin. I tell you that not even Solomon in all his splendor was dressed like one of these. If that is how God clothes the grass of the field, which is here today and tomorrow is thrown into the fire, will he not much more clothe you—you of little faith? So do not worry, saying, "What shall we eat?" or "What shall we drink?" or "What shall we wear?" For the pagans run after all these things, and your heavenly Father knows that you need them. But seek first his kingdom and his righteousness, and all these things will be given to you as well.

Matthew 6:25-33 NIV

BLYTHE AND CALYN DANIEL are a mother and daughter who love books and have a mission to strengthen relationships with families and friends.

BLYTHE is the coauthor of *Mended* and *I Love You, Mom!*, both of which she wrote with her mother, Dr. Helen McIntosh. She worked for Harper Collins Christian Publishing in marketing and publicity, and now enjoys her work as a literary agent. She lives in Colorado with her husband and three teenagers.

CALYN is a middle schooler and loves spending time with her friends and family, including older sister, Maris, and twin brother, William, who is also an author. She is a competitive gymnast and enjoys cooking. Calyn believes girls need to know who they are in Christ, how to navigate friend groups—especially when they change—and how to not lose sight of who God has made them to be.

To learn more about Harvest House books and
to read sample chapters, visit our website:

www.harvesthousepublishers.com

HARVEST HOUSE PUBLISHERS
EUGENE, OREGON